ur special

ur special

Advice for Humans from coolman_coffeedan

danny casale

A TarcherPerigee Book

tarcherperigee

An imprint of Penguin Random House LLC
penguinrandomhouse.com

Copyright © 2021 Danny Casale

TarcherPerigee with tp colophon is a registered trademark of Penguin
Random House LLC.

Most TarcherPerigee books are available at special quantity discounts
for bulk purchase for sales promotions, premiums, fund-raising,
and educational needs. Special books or book excerpts also can
be created to fit specific needs. For details, write: SpecialMarkets
@penguinrandomhouse.com.

Library of Congress Cataloging-in-Publication Data
Names: Casale, Danny, author, illustrator.
Title: Ur special: advice for humans from Coolman Coffeedan /
Danny Casale.
Description: [New York, New York]: TarcherPerigee,
Penguin Random House LLC, [2021]
Identifiers: LCCN 2020055754 (print) | LCCN 2020055755 (ebook) |
ISBN 9780593330104 (paperback) | ISBN 9780593330111 (ebook)
Subjects: LCSH: Conduct of life. | Self-realization. |
American wit and humor.
Classification: LCC BJ1589 .C374 2021 (print) | LCC BJ1589 (ebook) |
DDC 170/.44—dc23
LC record available at https://lccn.loc.gov/2020055754
LC ebook record available at https://lccn.loc.gov/2020055755

Barnes & Noble exclusive edition ISBN: 9780593421512

Printed in China

10 9 8 7 6 5 4 3 2 1

Book design by Silverglass

dedicated to
mom and dad

contents

ur special

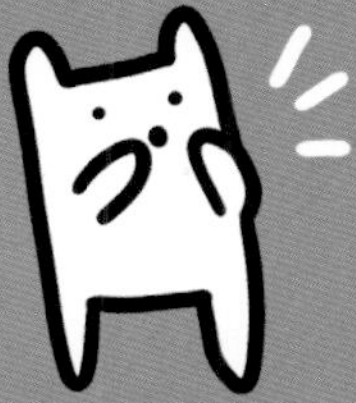

Before we start this book, did anybody lose this iguana?

He says his name is Alfred. He's excellent on the piano, a *master of the ivories,* some may say. He's also fluent in Spanish. Pretty impressive. I'm sure his owner is worried sick.

If you have any information, please call my house phone. My mom will probably answer. Tell her you're calling about Señor Iggy (the cool nickname I gave him) and she'll probably hand the phone over to me. Please call anytime besides Sundays. That's when she "meets up with the gals for brunch" or something.

Okay. Now we can start.

chapter 1
ur not alone

Hey! Thanks for picking up this book.

Things can get pretty lonely on the bookshelf. You wouldn't *believe* the amount of people that just pass by this book and don't even bother to flip through a few pages. But you did!

I mean, you probably even bought it. That's really cool. Thanks for buying me! You're a really cool person, so I should consider myself honored to be hanging out with you. That is, unless you're a book-robber who broke into the bookstore late at night, dodged a bunch of security lasers, and nabbed this incredible novel off the shelf without leaving a trace.

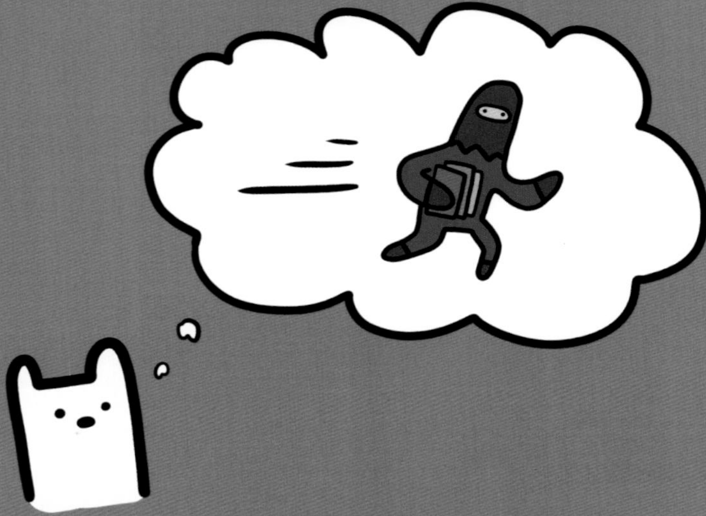

In that case, I definitely have a few questions. Like, how many books do you have to steal to be considered an official book-robber? Ten? Twenty? Does it say “certified book-robber” on your business card? How’s the book-robber job market looking nowadays? What was your biggest book heist? *Are there movies about book heists?* That would be pretty cool because you could dress up as a librarian super spy in disguise. I would totally watch that movie.

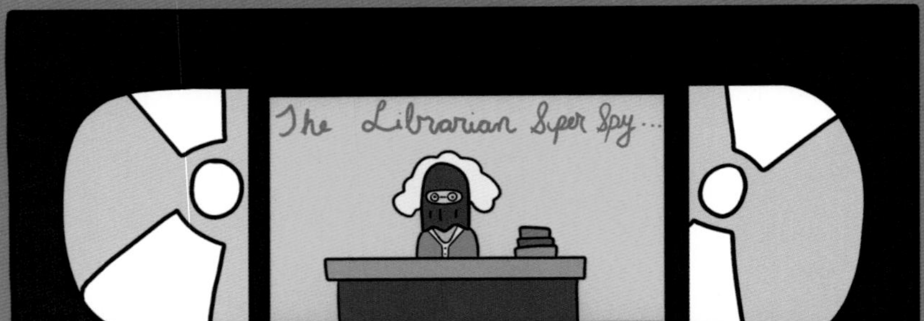
The Librarian Super Spy...

Anyways. I'm sure you're an upstanding citizen who paid for this book (or had someone who's really awesome buy it for you) and fully expect to enjoy the many life lessons I have in store for you!

Sometimes, life can be weird. Good-weird, bad-weird, or just plain weird-weird. There's no stopping life from *being* weird. The best we can do is be prepared for whatever weird stuff life is going to throw our way. It's not uncommon for life to surprise us with this weird stuff, and there's always an important lesson to be had. Oftentimes, we learn these important lessons from our mistakes. But it doesn't hurt to have a few lessons in your pocket *already* . . . "pre-mistake," if you will. It's like if you fall off a cliff, at least you have some bandages in your backpack to hold you over! Maybe that was a bad example? Please don't fall off any cliffs.

BUT WHAT IS A NAKED CAT-THING GOING TO TEACH ME? WHAT EXPERIENCE DOES IT EVEN HAVE? I'M A HUMAN WITH REAL HUMAN ISSUES... AND IT JUST TOLD ME THAT A BANDAGE IS THE CURE TO FALLING OFF A CLIFF! I WANT A REFUND.

Look. I may just be a naked cat-thing, but I like to think I have some wisdom to impart to your human brain. I have thoughts, feelings, fears, and insecurities too! You don't necessarily have to be human to *feel*. Just ask this houseplant!

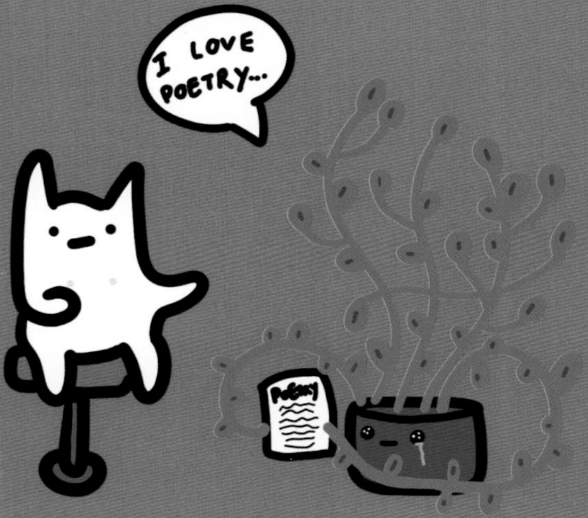
I LOVE POETRY...
POETRY

I know I may look different from you, but please don't think of me as different. When you meet someone new, all too often people will try to identify as many differences as they can. All that does is set you up to have way less friends! I'm sure we have a lot in common, actually. We probably both love delicious food and think puppies are adorable. Think of me as a friend who will guide you through the wonderful world of Life Lessons That You Definitely Should Learn Now Rather Than Later™. I would love for you to have a better understanding of what to do when life gets weird. Hopefully, when we're done spending our time together, you will have learned a thing or two more about yourself than if we didn't hang out at all!

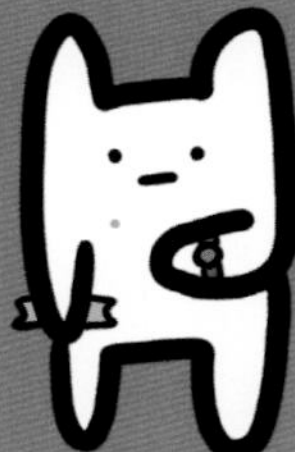

We should start *now*, though. I have plans to go to a movie and it starts soon, and I just *cannot* miss it. I bought these tickets like three months ago. Luckily we can talk as I make my way over to the cinema! Let's go!

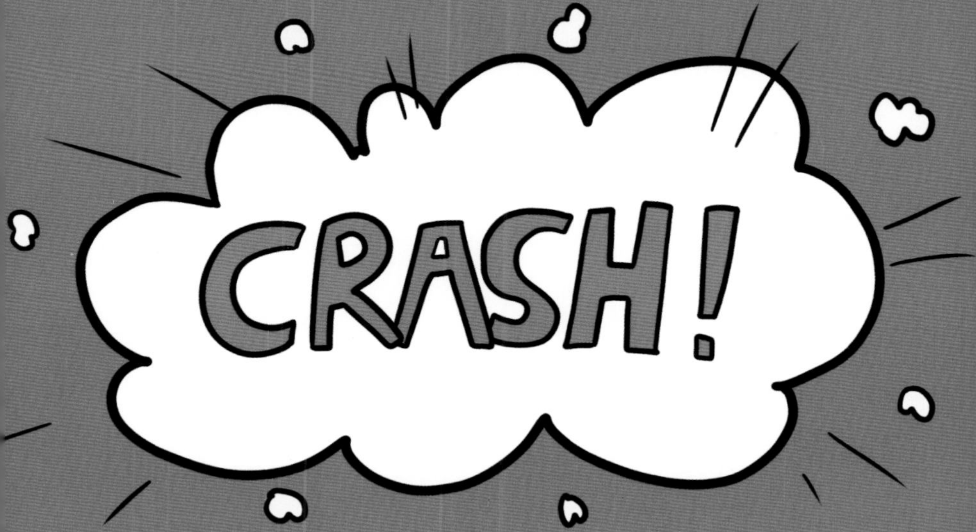
CRASH!

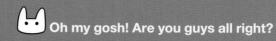 Oh my gosh! Are you guys all right?

Yes, thank you.

I told you we needed to get that broken computer chip checked out!

I was too nervous to call the mechanic! You know I have phone call anxiety!

Do you guys need help with directions or something? I have lessons to teach and a movie to catch so I really need to get going . . .

Yes . . . directions would be great.

We are lost and scared!

Well, when you think about it, it's okay to feel lost and scared sometimes . . .

No, like, we are literally millions of miles lost. Our home planet is in a different dimension.

Oh, okay. Lucky for you I have this Map of the Universe (patent pending).

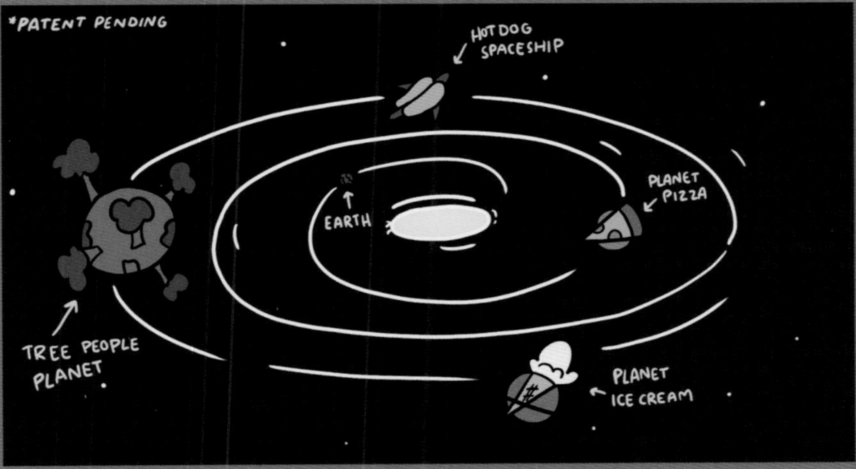
*PATENT PENDING
HOT DOG SPACESHIP
PLANET PIZZA
EARTH
TREE PEOPLE PLANET
PLANET ICE CREAM

Oh, I remember that planet! Everyone is a tree there.

Yes, we remember. You kept making tree puns.

Ha ha, nothin' beats comedy.

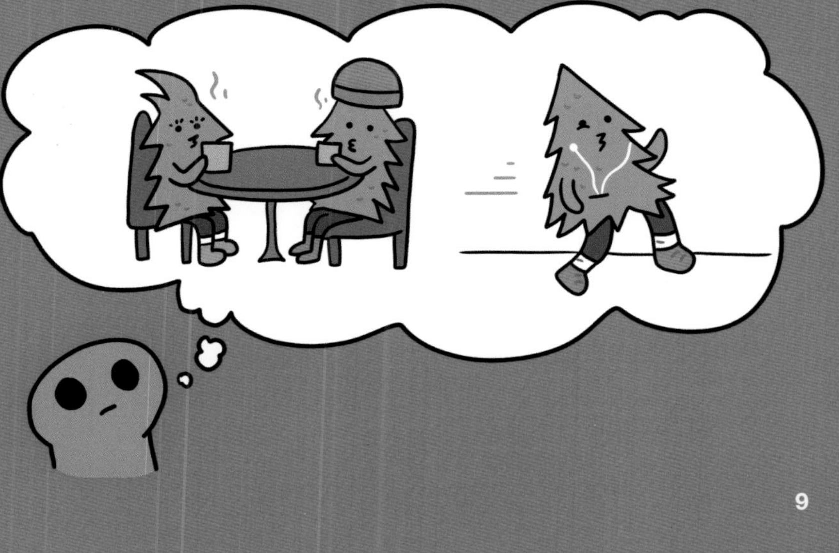

 You know, I never thought about how small Earth is. But looking at this map, I'm realizing that there's so much out there that I often don't think about. It makes all my problems look pretty small.

What problems do you have?! We are literally light-years from our home!

I don't know! I just get caught up in my own head. Sometimes I make my problems seem a lot bigger than they actually are. I should remind myself that there's so many creatures out there, dealing with their own stuff.

MEANWHILE, ON TREE PEOPLE PLANET...

I FEEL LIKE YOU JUST USE ME FOR MY BRANCHES!

We have a tendency to make our small problems bigger than they actually are. Everyone's going through something. But it's important to remember that what might seem like a big problem to you is tiny compared to someone else's. Not to say your problems aren't valid, but keeping other people in mind never hurts and is a great way to keep everything in perspective.

Anyways, it looks like you're going to wanna go *that* way. Follow the North Star and make a left at the Little Dipper. If you see Planet Pizza you've gone too far.

Thanks for the directions and the free life lesson!

Yeah, I feel guided in more ways than one!

Let's blow this Popsicle planet, boys!

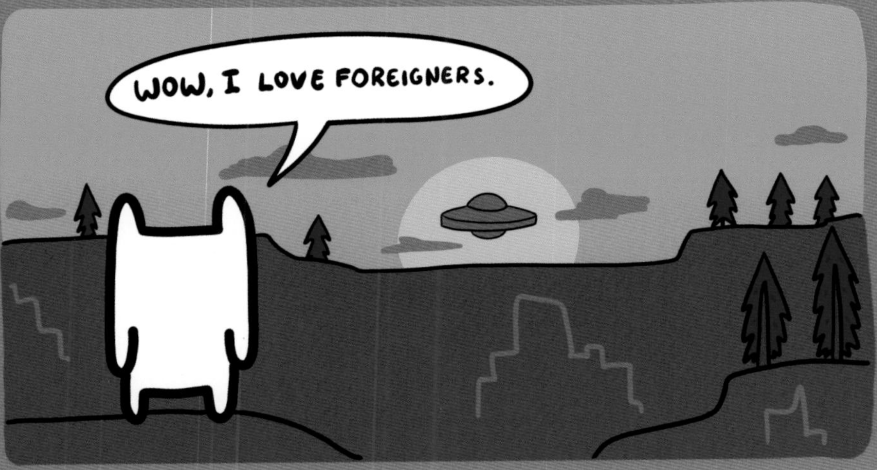
WOW, I LOVE FOREIGNERS.

chapter 2
ur not ugly

So yeah. This movie is going to be great. It's an indie film about love or whatever. I'm going because when I see a really good movie, it feels like it has read my mind. That's an amazing feeling.

I like going to the movies alone because I really enjoy the quality time with myself. I feel like alone time isn't nearly as socially acceptable as it should be. People think they should feel sad for those who are alone, like it's a weird thing to do. Don't get me wrong, I love when I get to see the people I care about, but I also love being alone. You get to learn about yourself and think about things you never thought about before. It's like going on a date with yourself!

Even though it's just me, I usually buy two tickets. The only reason I do that is because I usually order a bag of popcorn so large that it legally qualifies as a small child. I would invite you, but I need that extra seat for my popcorn. I tried getting a smaller size, but it always disappears before the movie even starts, so—

"Excuse me!"

Whoa. Uh. Hey.

I couldn't help but notice that you walked right past me without saying anything. No hello. No wink. Not even a nod!

Uh, sorry . . .

Is it because I'm ugly?

No way! It's not that. I just had some stuff on my mind . . .

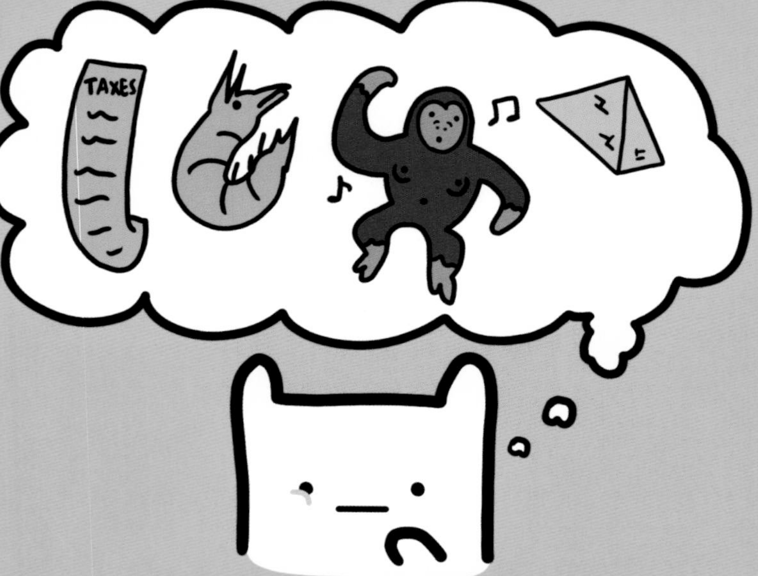
TAXES

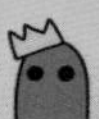 **Oh. It’s okay. Sorry if I came off as rude. Sometimes I just have really bad days where my self-confidence feels like it’s below zero. It’s no one’s fault in particular, just me getting in my own head. On days like today I can’t even bring myself to look anybody in the eye. I also think everybody is making fun of me, even though they probably aren’t. I know it sounds ridiculous, but I would pay a million dollars just to have some amount of confidence. No matter how hard I try, I still feel like the ugliest girl in the world.**

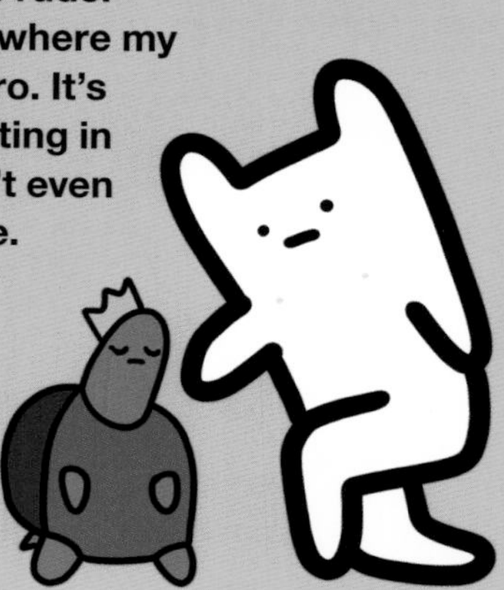

Hey. It's totally normal to feel like that sometimes. Occasionally having a bad day or two is just what we signed up for when we were put on this planet. It even makes us stronger once we overcome those bad days. Recently I was staring at myself in the mirror for what felt like hours, just because I had a pimple on my forehead. It felt like my world was falling apart, even though it was such a microscopic issue. I eventually got over it because I saw a cloud that looked like a cowboy hat. However, feeling like you're having too many of these bad days is a problem and needs to be taken care of properly.

For example, what do you do when you fall off a cliff?

What?!

Erm . . . never mind. How about . . . what do you do when you fall off your bike and scrape your knee?

Hmm . . . lie there for hours crying, hoping a pack of wolves finds me and takes me into their family as their very own?

17

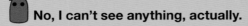 What? No! You find help. You wash the wound and put a bandage on your knee. You address the thing that hurts so that it heals and gets better! That's what you need to do with your self-confidence. Learn to identify when you feel this way so that you are prepared to handle it properly. Maybe it's through keeping a journal of your thoughts. Maybe it's through bringing it up to a friend or family member you trust. However you do it, you need to remember to put a bandage on it.

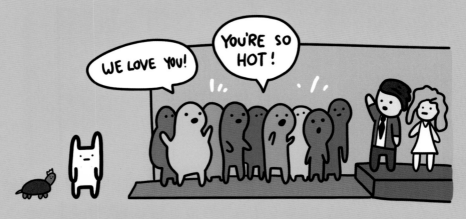

See those gorgeous celebrities?

No, I can't see anything, actually.

Oh . . . Now can you see?

Yeah. Thanks.

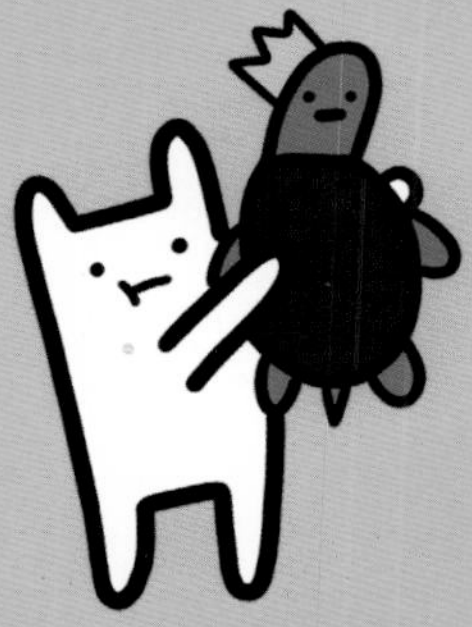

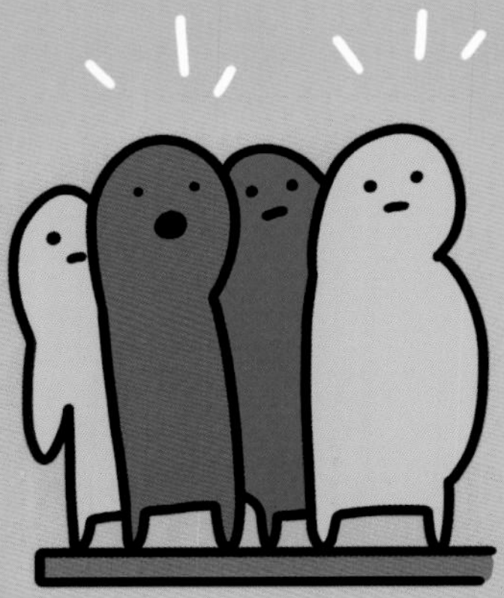

Don't they look happy? I mean, what more could they ask for? They got good looks, money, fame, and $7,000 flip-flops. Everyone in this crowd loves them!

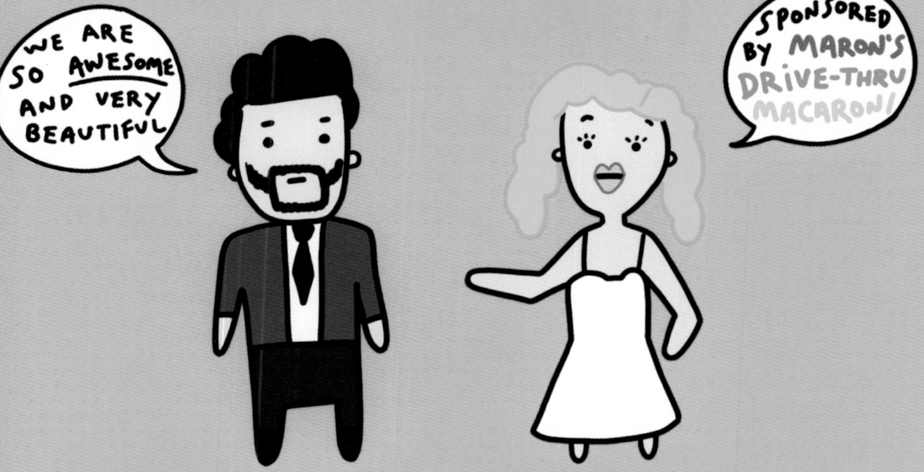
WE ARE SO AWESOME AND VERY BEAUTIFUL
SPONSORED BY MARON'S DRIVE-THRU MACARON!

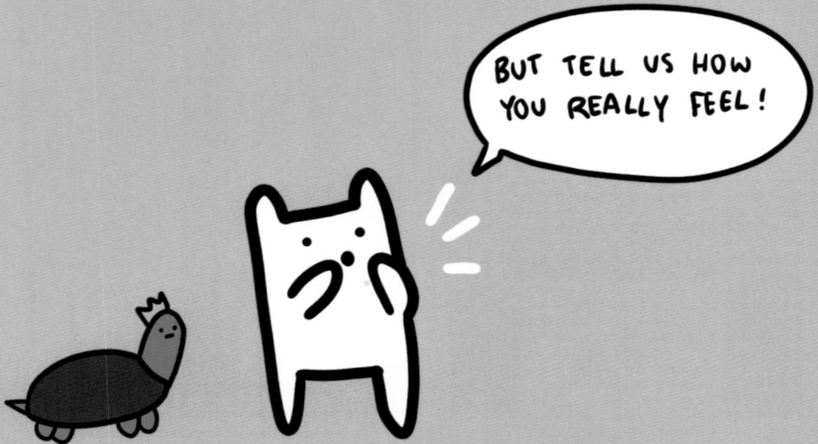
BUT TELL US HOW YOU REALLY FEEL!

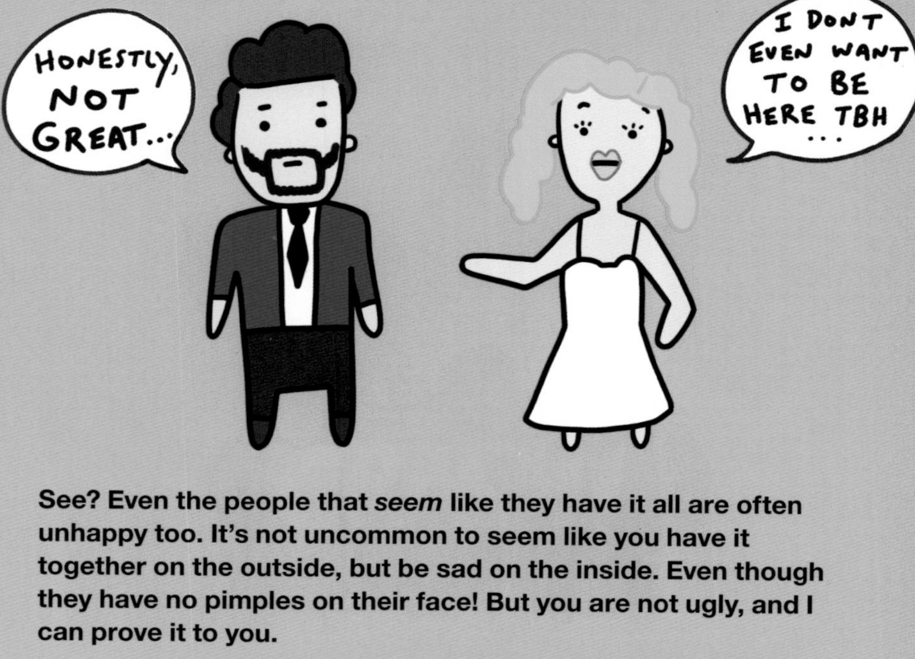
HONESTLY, NOT GREAT...
I DONT EVEN WANT TO BE HERE TBH ...

See? Even the people that *seem* like they have it all are often unhappy too. It's not uncommon to seem like you have it together on the outside, but be sad on the inside. Even though they have no pimples on their face! But you are not ugly, and I can prove it to you.

" COOL FEATURES "

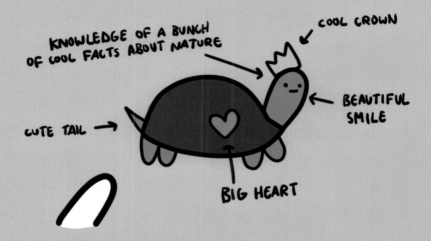

KNOWLEDGE OF A BUNCH OF COOL FACTS ABOUT NATURE

COOL CROWN

CUTE TAIL →

BEAUTIFUL SMILE

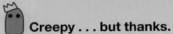 BIG HEART

And look, I even made you my phone screen background!

Creepy . . . but thanks.

What I'm saying is . . . there's so many beautiful things about you. You just have to stop being so critical of yourself. Accept yourself for who you are. Notice all the incredible qualities that you have, even though you *think* you don't have any. That's just your rotten thoughts trying to trick you, and you shouldn't pay any mind to those. Instead, pay attention to the positive thoughts that you've been ignoring for so long. They are there, you just have to listen to them. They've been desperately trying to get in touch with you!

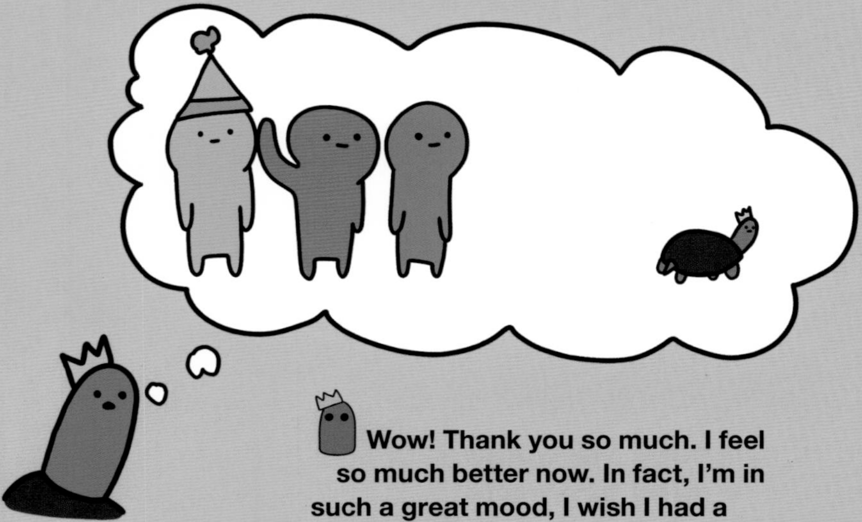

Wow! Thank you so much. I feel so much better now. In fact, I'm in such a great mood, I wish I had a way to celebrate accordingly . . .

Sigh . . . Do you wanna come see a movie with me?

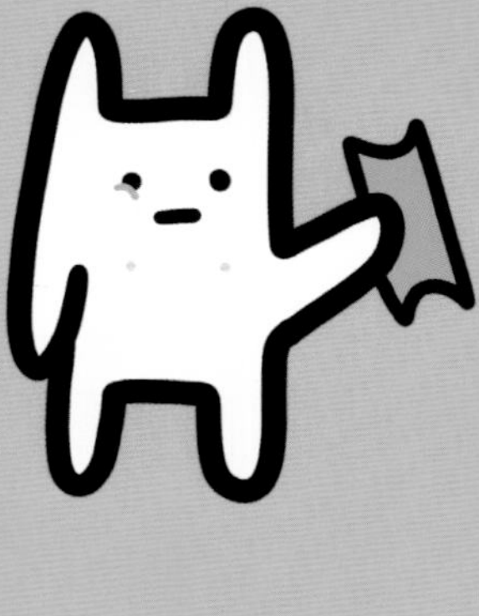

Sure! Sounds like fun.

Sometimes, you sacrifice something you really wanted for someone you care about. It's tough, but it's usually the right thing to do. In this case, the right thing to do was to give up my extra-popcorn-cinema-seat-reserving ticket for a small, crown-wearing turtle with low-self-esteem issues. But who wouldn't do that, am I right?

Hey, can you change your phone background now?

Yeah, I thought you might say that.

chapter 3

ur totally making cereal wrong

Okay. So. I hope to inspire a small amount of change through this connection with you. Whether it's about self-awareness, mental health, or your perspective on others. But if I don't, can I at least make something perfectly clear before we move any further in this *delightful masterpiece* of a book?

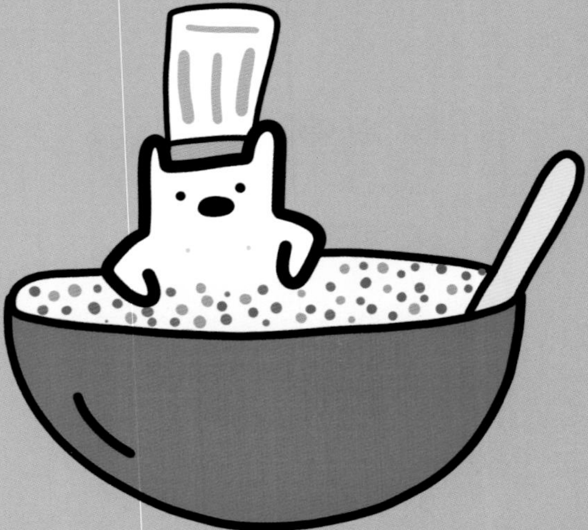

THERE.

IS.

ONLY.

ONE.

WAY.

TO.

PREPARE.

DELICIOUS.

CEREAL.

I can't believe I'm even saying this right now. The fact that anybody even doubts this for a moment is mind-boggling to me! I've explained this in detail one too many times to those who simply do not understand . . . so I'm putting an end to it and laying it out once and for all. Mamma mia!

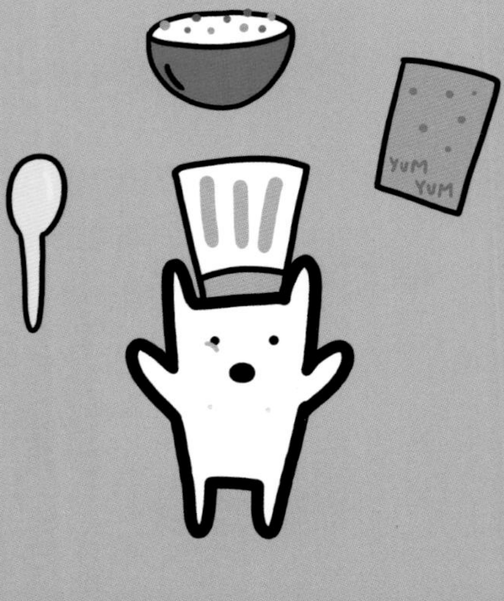
YUM
YUM

THE CORRECT CEREAL INGREDIENT ORDER IS AS FOLLOWS:

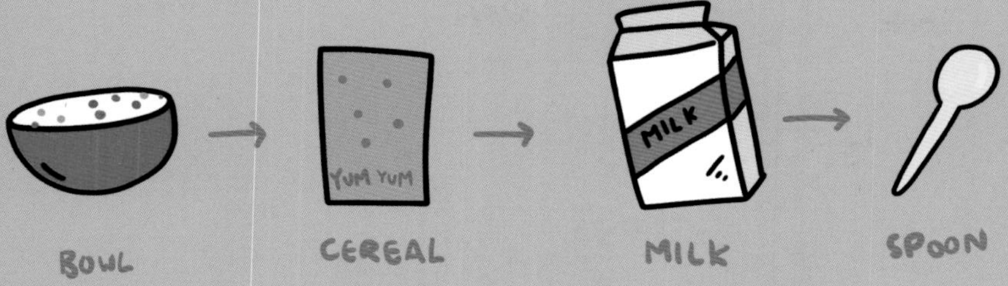
YUM YUM
MILK
BOWL
CEREAL
MILK
SPOON

There is simply no debating that this is the universally accepted way to properly prepare a delicious bowl of cereal. Like, how do you eat it any other way? There is no other way!

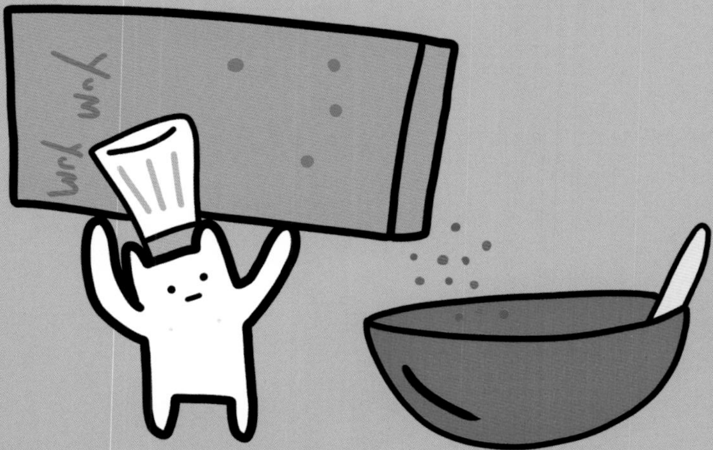
YUM YUM

SOME INCORRECT CEREAL INGREDIENT ORDERS:

🥣 → MILK → YUM YUM → 🥄 → OH GOD NO

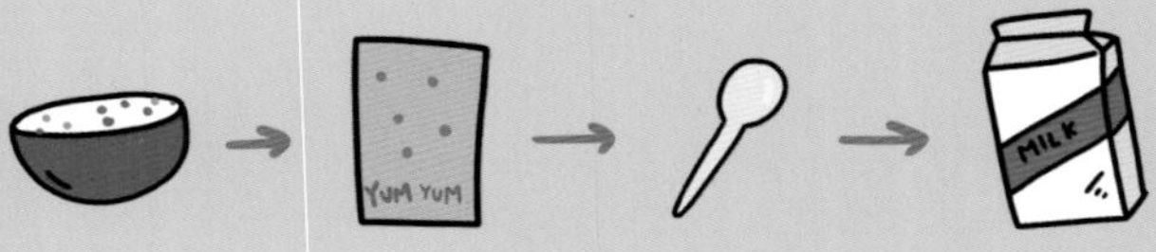

🥣 → YUM YUM → 🥄 → MILK → DEFINITELY NOT

MORE INCORRECT CEREAL INGREDIENT ORDERS:

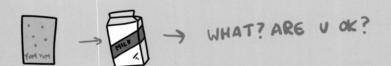

YUM YUM → MILK → WHAT? ARE U OK?

LETTUCE → TOMATO → FORK → SALAD. YOU MADE A SALAD.

I'm all for freedom of speech. I'm not one to force others to do anything they don't want to. And you're allowed to prepare your bowl of cereal however you please.

But just please know that if you continue to prepare cereal incorrectly, the universe might literally collapse into a black hole, and we will all die.

Also know that I am right.

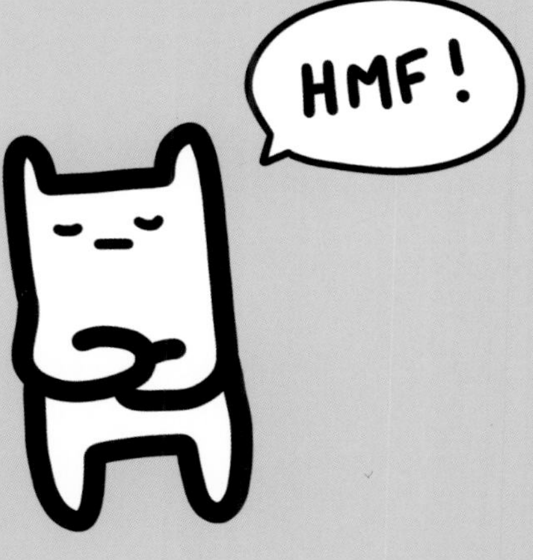
HMF!

chapter 4
ur missing someone

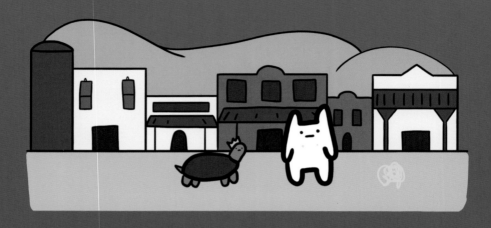

 . . . and that's how I got my crown!

 Wow. I can't believe you rap-battled Zeus and won.

Yep!

Do you hear that?

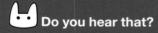 Do you hear that?

 It sounds like someone's crying . . .

 Hey there! What's wrong?

I lost something I can't replace. I am so sad. Beep boop.

I'm so sorry to hear that. What did you lose?

I lost my arms.

Oh my!

They were the best arms a robot could ask for. They took good care of me. They had AI capabilities, a personality of their own, and a great sense of humor.

The right arm was sensitive, but funny. The left arm was a master chef. I ate amazing sandwiches and laughed all day, every day. They were my role models, my loved ones, my everything. But now, they are gone. I miss them so much. Boop.

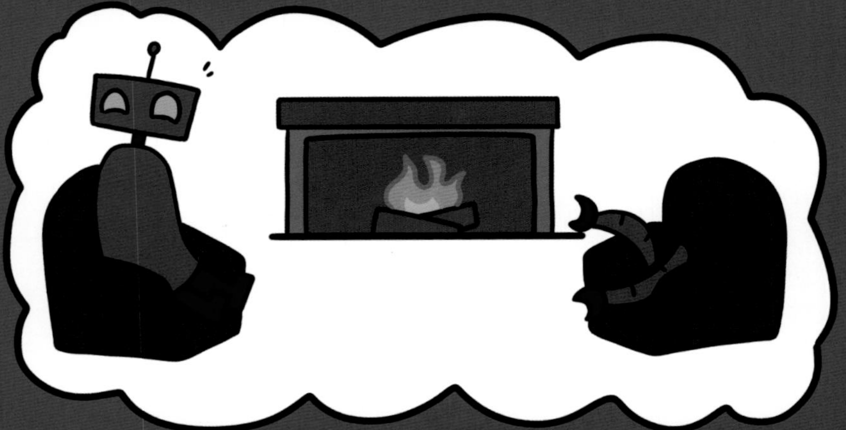

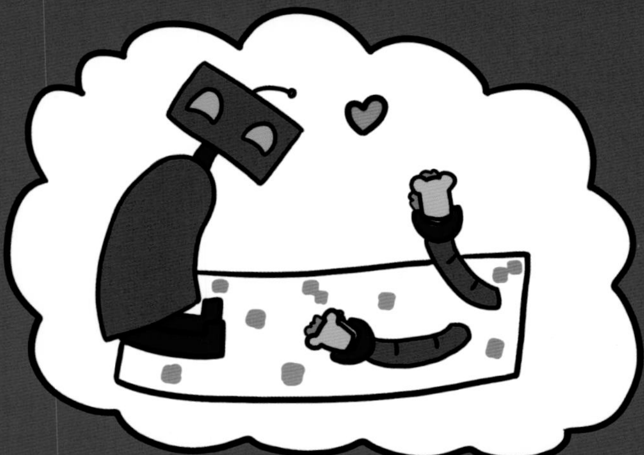

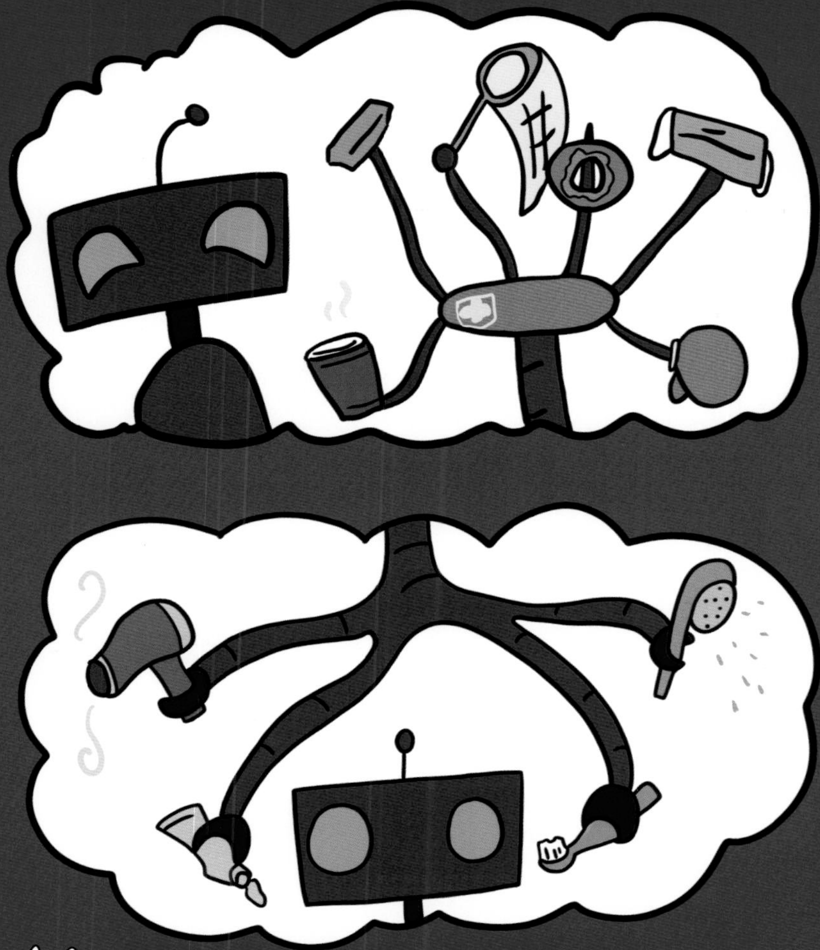

I'm very sorry for your loss, Mr. Robot.

I wish I had more time with them. I would do anything to have just five more minutes with those precious arms. They were my whole world. I have no idea what to do without them. I'm sad, nervous, and scared of what my life will be without them.

 That must be tough. I can tell you miss them very much. Losing someone you love can feel like you literally lost a part of *you*. And as tough as that is, missing someone means you have been given the chance to LOVE someone . . . and not everyone gets the chance to love somebody.

The fact that you miss someone means that you had amazing times with them. Which is a million times better than not having had amazing times at all. It's okay to miss someone because that means you have *loved*. And there's nothing wrong with that. Is there?

Nope.

I do have amazing memories with them, ones that I'll cherish forever. I appreciate the time I had with them, and I know they would want me to continue living my life too. It will take some time to feel normal again, but having people like you offering comfort really makes it all feel a little bit easier for me. Thank you.

 Of course! Talking through times like these with your friends is the most important thing ever. I know you felt like you wanted to be alone and cry by yourself. It's not uncommon for someone to feel so upset that they push everyone away. But communicating with people who care about you is also very important for the healing process. You have a lot of emotions and thoughts going through your robot head right now, and we're happy to lend an ear to listen.

Yeah! I lost my crown a few months ago. It was really rough. Some days were easier than others and I cried a lot.

But your crown is right there, on your head!

Yes. I eventually found it again, which made me so happy. But I also understand that maybe you won't have the chance to see your arms again. I can't do much except do my best to be here for you in your time of need. So I will use my own experiences, although limited, to try to understand your feelings and do my absolute best to help you through this difficult time.

IF FOUND PLEASE RETURN TO CRYING TURTLE.

We are here for you, Robot!

 BEEP BOOP!

37

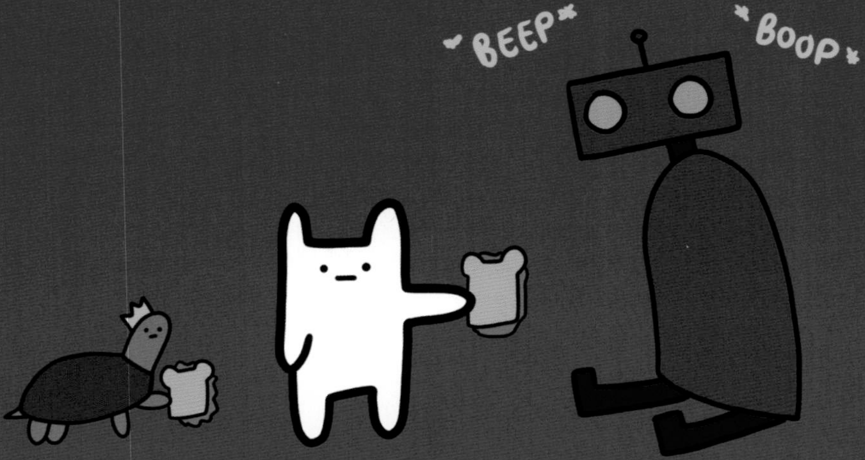

BEEP
BOOP

Wow. Thank you. I really appreciate that. Just you two being here already helps my mood. Beep boop!

Wanna come see a movie with us?

Whoa, I'd love to!

It's going to be so fun! Right?

Uh . . . yeah! It will be great. The movie starts soon, so let's get a move on!

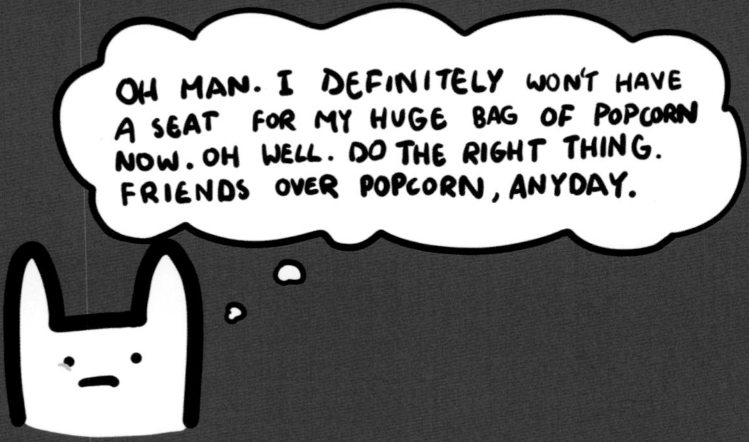

OH MAN. I DEFINITELY WON'T HAVE A SEAT FOR MY HUGE BAG OF POPCORN NOW. OH WELL. DO THE RIGHT THING. FRIENDS OVER POPCORN, ANYDAY.

chapter 5
u got time

Going on walks is a really great way to pass the time. Not enough people do it for the pleasure of it! Everyone thinks it's boring and slow, but if you have some time with nowhere to go in particular, it's a fantastic way to clear your mind and get some exercise. One time I started walking and didn't stop until I fell asleep in a cornfield somewhere. The only thing that woke me up was the *oinks* from a family of pigs. It was the most fun morning I've ever had.

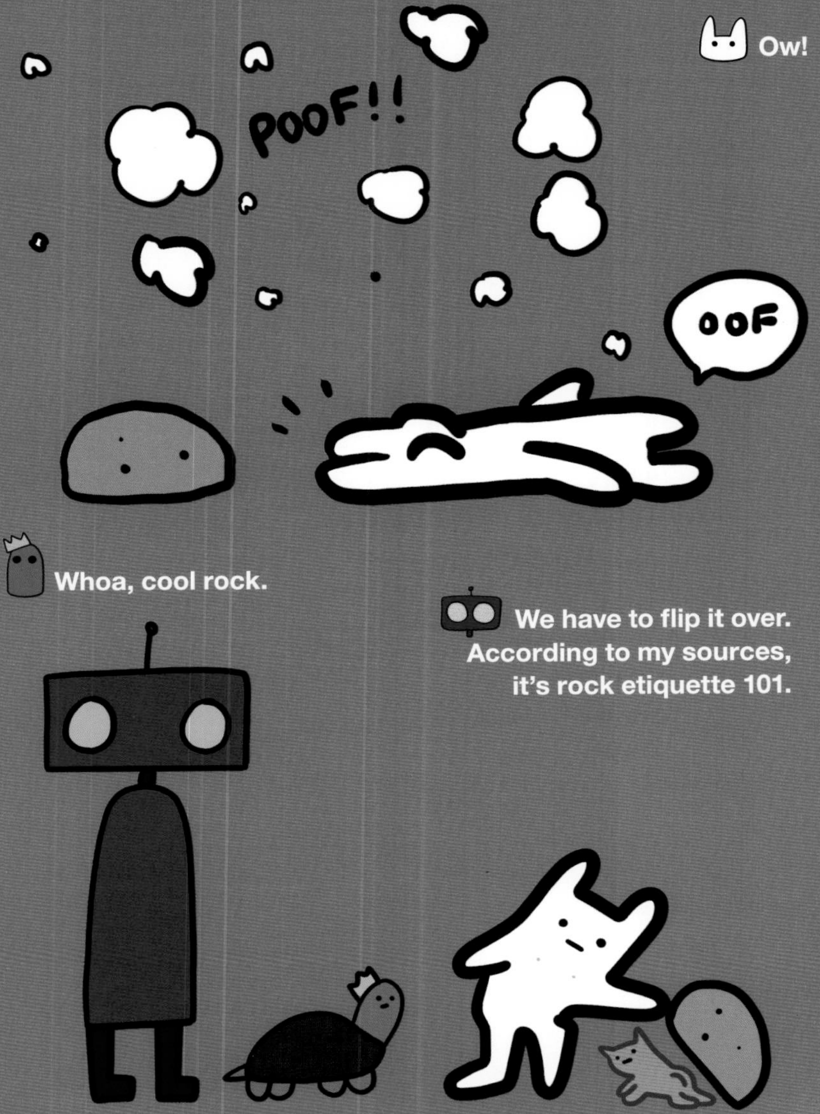
Ow!
POOF!!
OOF
Whoa, cool rock.
We have to flip it over. According to my sources, it's rock etiquette 101.

 Whoa! Where are your manners? Don't you know to knock first?!

 I didn't think we needed to knock a rock . . .

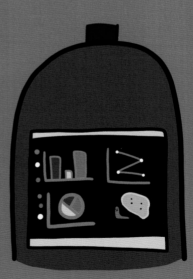 **It's true. Rock knocking isn't listed anywhere in the entirety of the Rock Etiquette Database.**

Oh—correction. I just gawked a doc that was chock-full of rock-knocking talk. The little red man is right.

Okay, okay . . . sorry for not knocking your rock, Little Red Man!

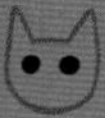 It’s fine, it’s fine. I suppose it was time for me to wrap up my 7th nap of the day. And I suppose I do have some time until my 8th . . . Say, wanna see my cool new bike?

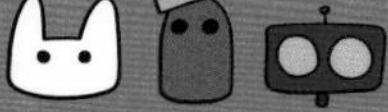 Definitely!

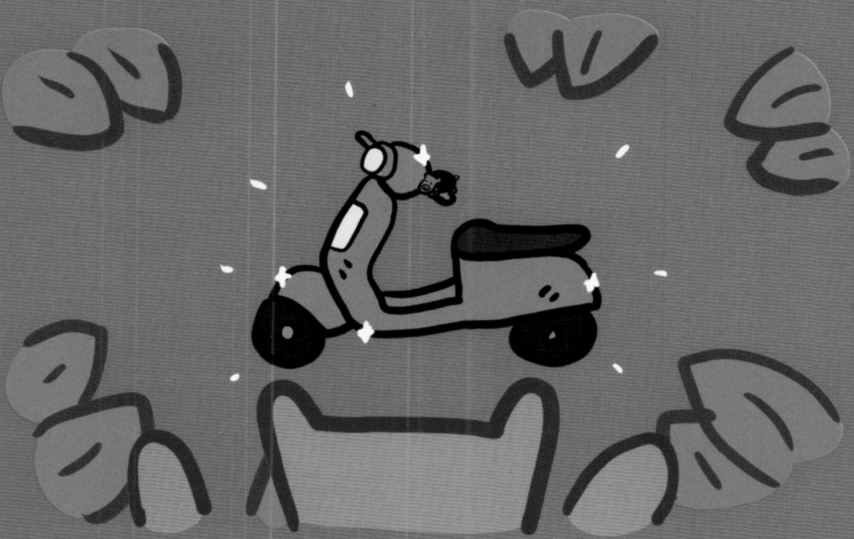

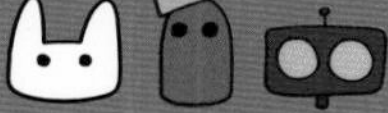 Whoa! Cool! Nice!

MR. DEVIL'S COOL ITALIAN MOPED

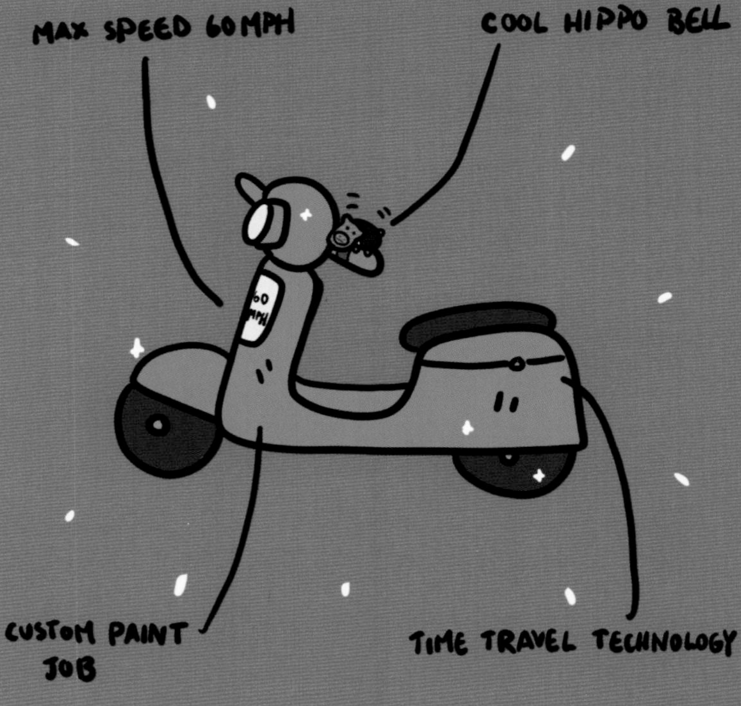
MAX SPEED 60 MPH
COOL HIPPO BELL
60 MPH
CUSTOM PAINT JOB
TIME TRAVEL TECHNOLOGY

It's an Italian moped. Fully decked out. Just had it imported last week. Custom paint job, max speed of 60 mph, technology built into the motherboard that's capable of traveling through time, a cool little bell shaped like a hippo . . .

Wait . . . what did you just say?

Yeah, it's a hippo, but dressed in a tuxedo. Super funny, right?

No! Not that! You said it was capable of TIME TRAVEL?!

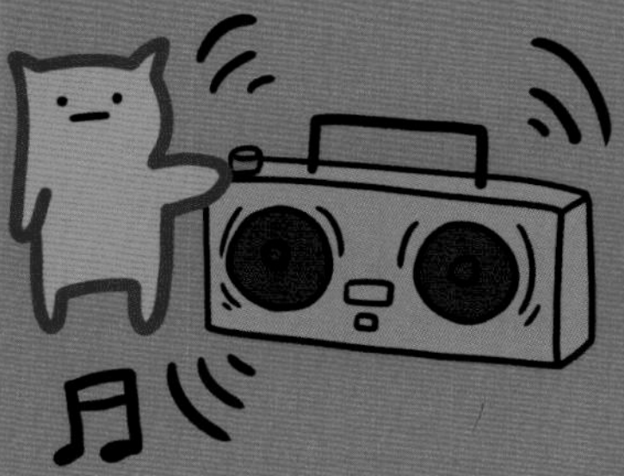

Ah yes. Ehem.

Hop on its leather seat,

Ring the hippo bell thrice,

And see your future with your very own eyes.

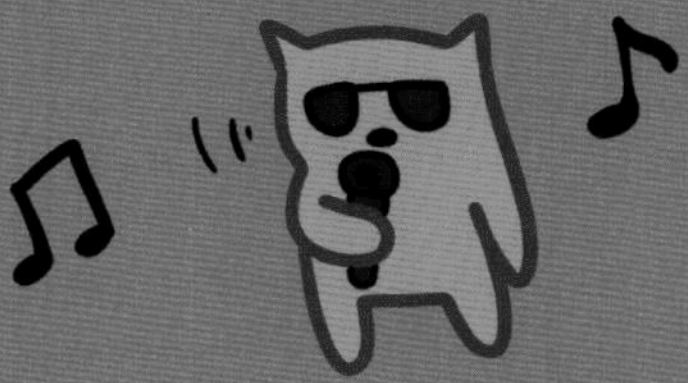

But beware of what you see,

For your future may or may not be what you'd expect it to be.

Will you be a chef?

How about be a lawyer?

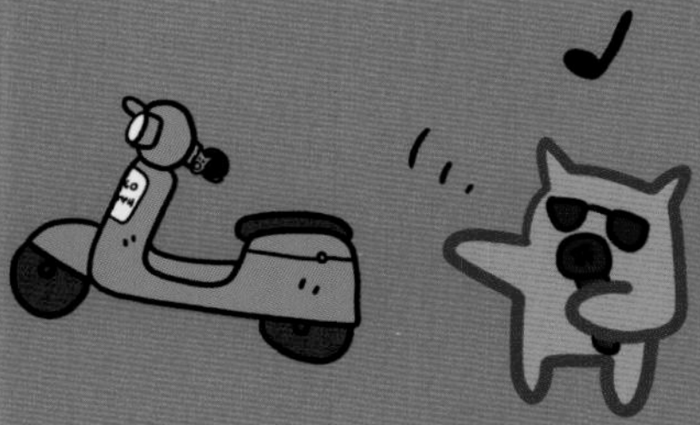

Or maybe a magical wizard who can communicate with oysters?

The choice is yours, but please choose soon . . .

For the chance to peek into your future

Only comes once in a blue moon.

Also, my next nap is in fifteen minutes.

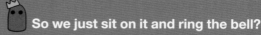

So we just sit on it and ring the bell?

Yes! Did you listen to anything I just said?

Not really. I'm more into jazz.

Oh! Why didn't you just say so?

SCOOBA
DO BA DEE
DODOOO...
WHAT'S
DA FUTURE
GOT IN
STORE
FOR U...

Okay! Okay! No jazz! We get it.

 I fear if we go into the future, we might not like what we see. What if I grow up to be a rotten old toaster? Or a blender? Or a fork?!

Why are you so fixated on kitchen appliances?

Yeah, maybe this isn't such a great idea. My nervous stomach is acting up . . .

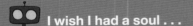 Come on, guys! It could be fun! Maybe you're millionaires in the future! Or supermodels! The amazing possibilities are endless . . .

This isn't some sort of devil soul-selling deal, is it?

My soul is worth way more than my curiosity!!!

I wish I had a soul . . .

What? No, I just want to show you my bike. That's actually pretty insulting.

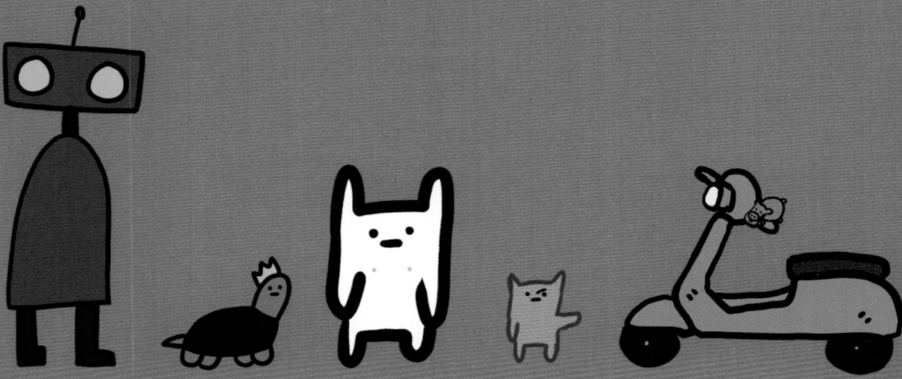

Oh. Sorry. It's just, usually when a devil makes a mysterious offer in the middle of the forest, it means you want to trade it for our souls. Sorry we judged you, I guess.

Ugh. You people are all the same. Just hop on . . .

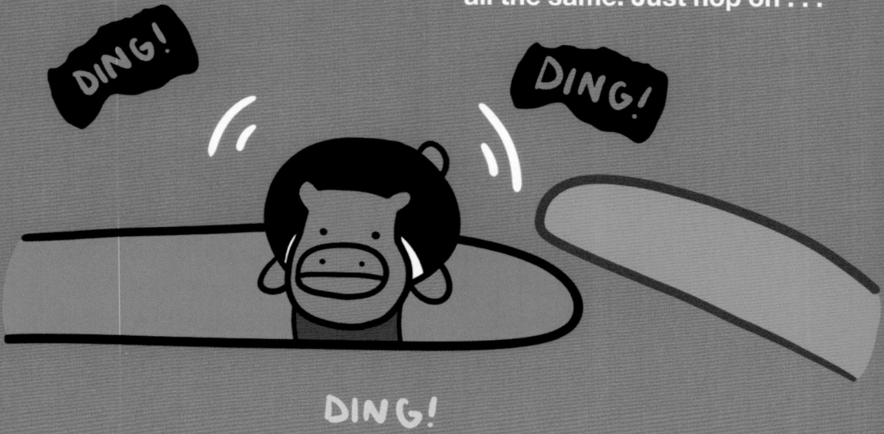
DING!
DING!
DING!

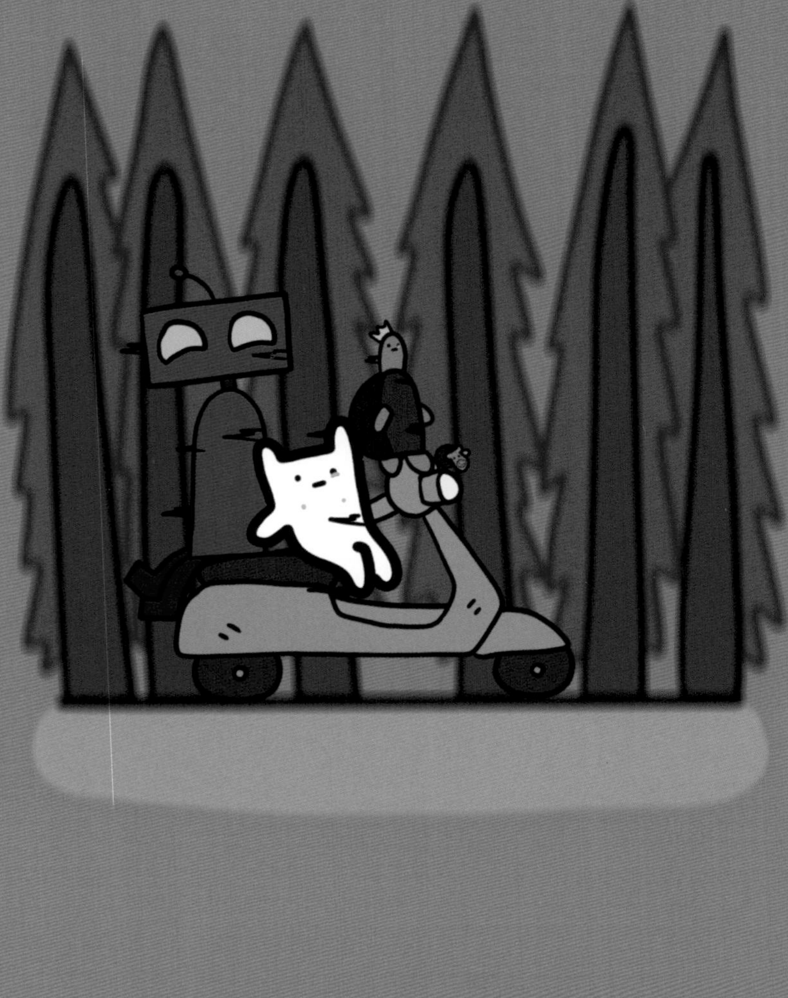

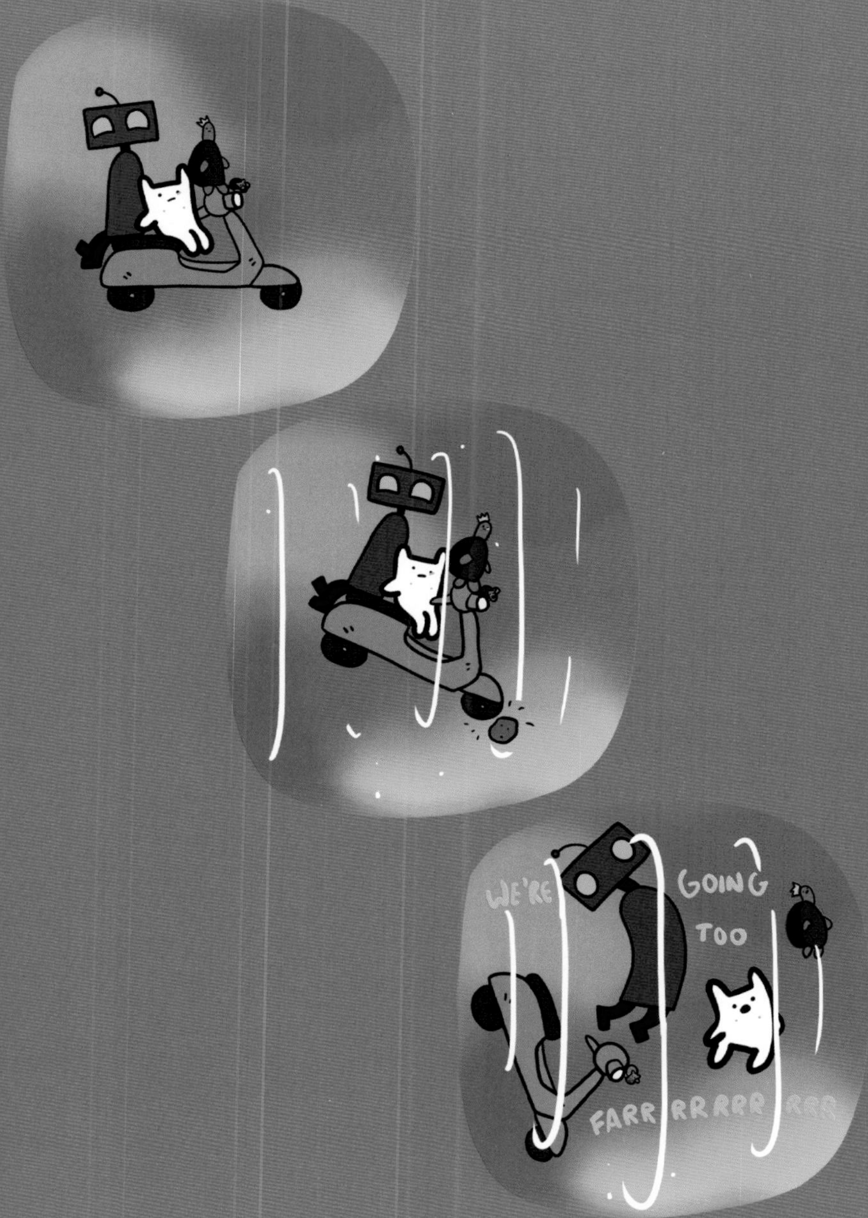
WE'RE GOING TOO
FARRRRRRRRRR

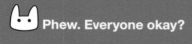Phew. Everyone okay?

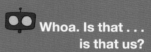Whoa. Is that . . .
is that us?

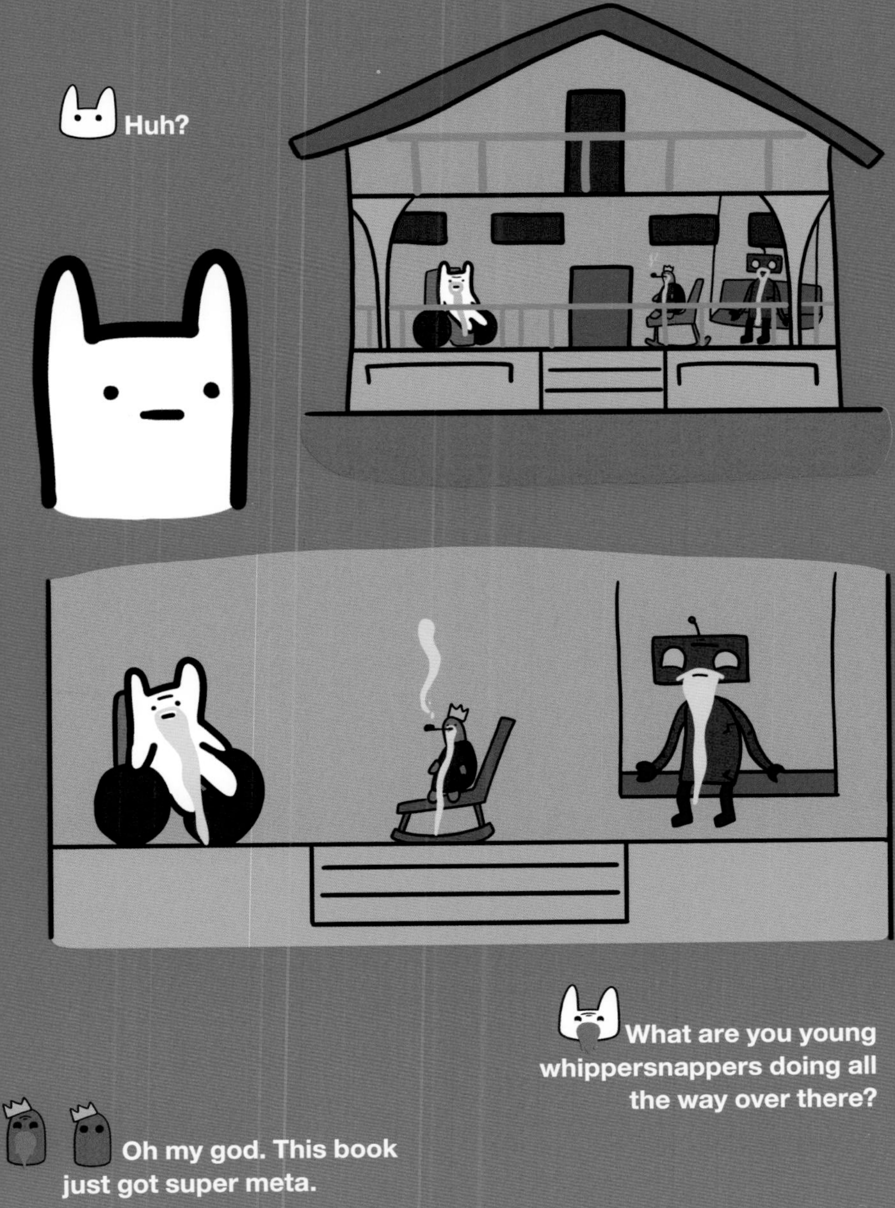
Huh?
What are you young whippersnappers doing all the way over there?
Oh my god. This book just got super meta.

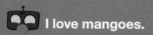 Come over here and keep us some company, why don't ya?

Yeah. Come here, gang!

I love mangoes.

Ah, we've been waiting for you.
Wow, I used to be so handsome.

You guys aren't freaked out that the younger version
of yourselves just time traveled here on a mysterious
magical bike given to us by a devil in the middle of nowhere?

Hah. I remember when I
asked that many questions.
Time really does fly.

To be honest, nothing really surprises
us anymore, young ones. The things we lived through
would make your head spin. We witnessed people who
traveled to Jupiter, experienced the invention of spicy water,
and lived through the Great Lamp War a few decades ago.

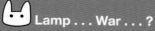 Lamp . . . War . . . ?

Yeah. It was historic. A bunch of lamps fought a bunch of moths for their right to personal space. Wild times.

I love mangoes!

Erm . . . why do I keep saying that?

A few nuts and bolts got loosened up. A few circuit boards aren't as fresh as they used to be. But it's only because he had a ton of fun along the way!

I love mangoes . . .

Whoa! Old-you has arms!

I can't believe it. I have arms again in the future?

Well, yes. Somewhere along the way, you found yourself a new pair of arms. Life is full of surprises. They are by no means the old arms you knew. They are very different and will never totally replace your old ones. But they still make you happy, and you were overdue for some happiness.

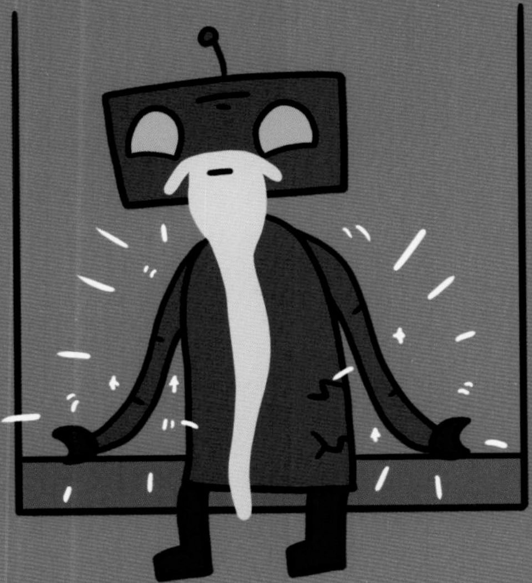

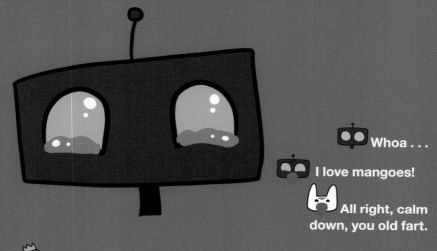

Whoa . . .

I love mangoes!

All right, calm
down, you old fart.

What about me? What happened
to me as I grew up? Did I get really
confident? Did I never feel sad again??

Well . . . no. No one ever feels
amazing *all the time*. If that were the case,
we wouldn't know how to feel anything else.
And who wants to feel nothing?
That sounds like a boring life to me.

You are making,
like, zero sense, girl.

Look. I never did figure out how to feel
entirely confident all the time. If I did, I would go
down in the history books as a legend. I would
be rich and famous for telling the secret of
how to achieve such a thing. But in reality,
such a goal is unattainable.

You're really bumming me out here.

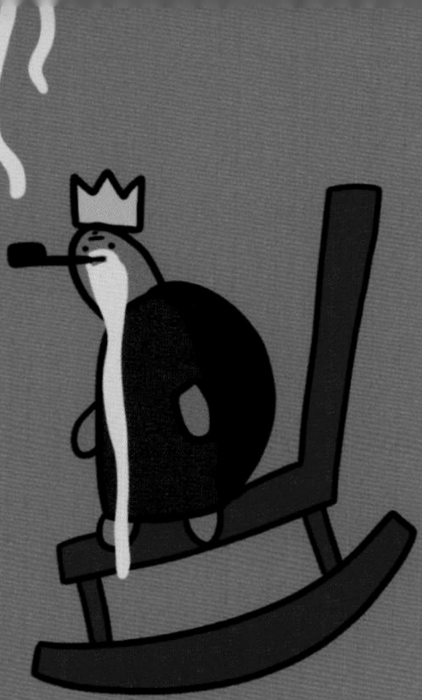

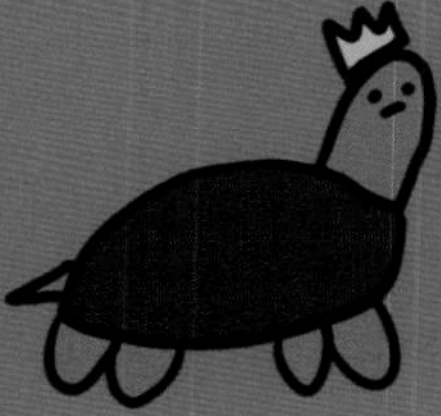

But I *did* figure out how to become the best version of myself that I possibly could. As I grew, I learned to love myself more and more. Sure, some days were tougher than others. There were very difficult times along the way too. But they only made me stronger. I am a million times more confident today than I was when I was your age. But it's only because I worked on myself. The more time I spent with myself, the more I learned that I'm actually a pretty cool turtle.

That's . . . really great to hear. Thank you for the advice. I'm pretty smart.

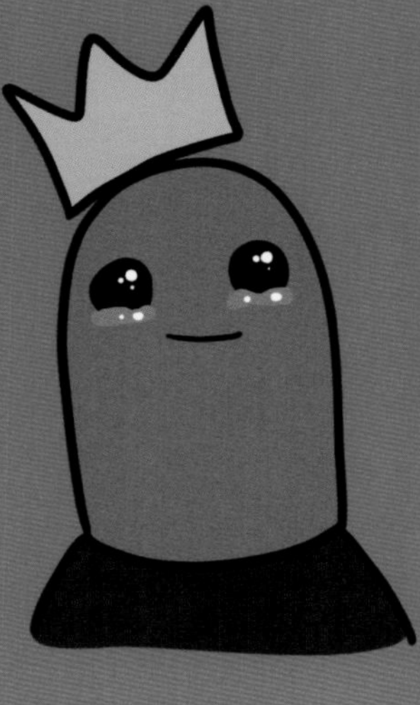

Yes, I am.

Hey! What about me! Where's my extremely profound life advice?

Listen, man, I just vibed along the way. Helped people when I could. Ate great food. I danced. Spent time with everyone I loved.

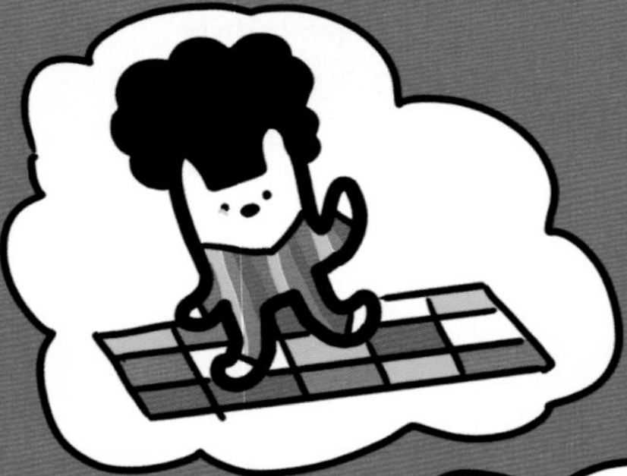

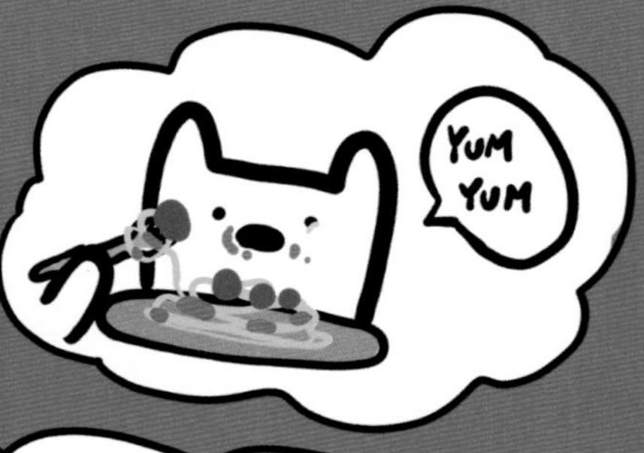
YUM YUM

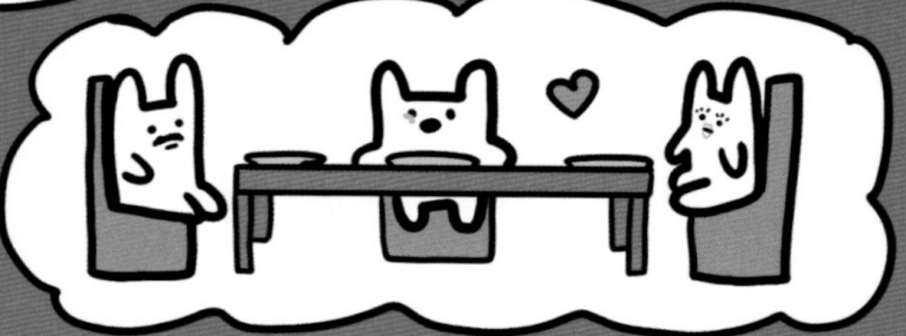

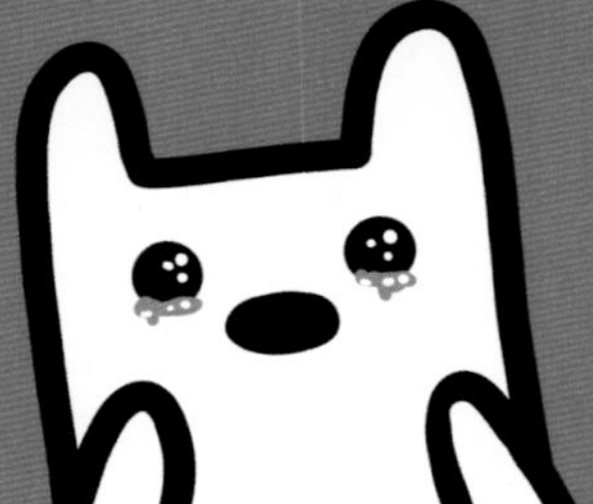

Now I sit here, old as heck, and couldn't be more content with how I spent my time. If you ask me, that's true happiness.

Wow, you're right. I vow to live my life to the fullest so that when I'm old I can have a really cool beard and sit on my butt all day!

Don’t forget about the pièce de résistance . . .

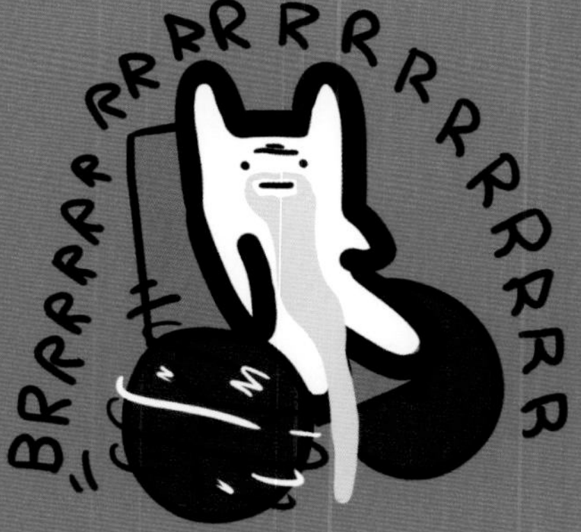

BRRRRRRRRRRRRRRRRRRRRRRR

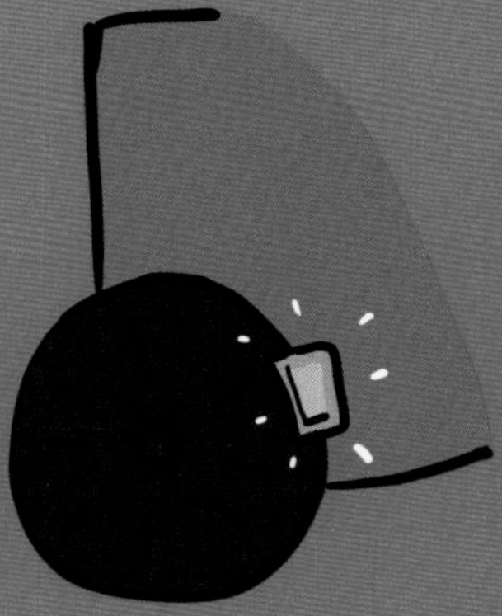

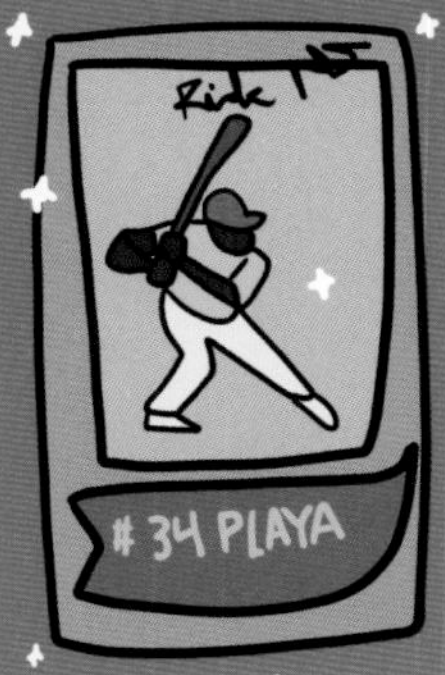

Rick
34 PLAYA

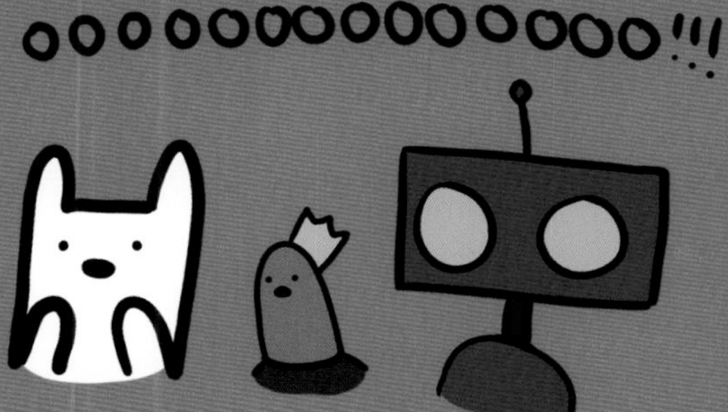

OOOOOOOOOOOOOOOO!!!

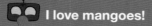 Really, all we're trying to say is to not worry so much. There will always be someone you'll be missing or something you'd wish was better. That's just what we all signed up for. But being in a constant state of worry means you're never in the state of living in the *present*.

That's right. Focusing on living in the now is the most valuable thing one can do. All too often someone wastes all their energy thinking about the past, or focusing too much on the future. When really all we have is the *now*. And we might as well enjoy it!

I love mangoes!

Wow. This is great. I have so many other questions for you guys, I don't know where to start!

Yeah, can you guys tell us winning lottery numbers? That would be so cool.

For sure. You got a pen? Here's every winning lottery number for the next eighty years . . .

Okay, so, 7—

POOF!

Welcome back! How was it? Did you see the vegetables that never expire? Crazy . . .

What did you do?!! We were just about to be filthy stinking rich!!

Sorry, no refunds.

I can't believe I met my older self. I seemed so happy.

I'm glad I eventually find some new arms to make me happy. I seemed a little crazy, but he's not wrong. I really do love mangoes.

Yeah. It seems like everything really does work out in the end.

Ah, so you all learned the lesson.

Lesson?! Hey, that's my job!

The lesson that life is short. Life can zoom by as quick as a bicycle zooms through the trees. So why not enjoy it? Use your time to its fullest extent. Use it to dance! Use it to love! Use it to grow! For one day you will be old, looking back on your life. And you want to be smiling while you do so.

Did you ever ride that bike to visit your future self and get perspective like we did?

There wouldn't be a point. Devils don't age. I'm actually 3,677 years old. I also use this amazing moisturizer. I don't look a day past twenty!

CRASH!

Wow. Good for you.

Are you kidding me?

ARE YOU KIDDING ME?
HEY, WANNA SEE MY BIKE?

chapter 6
u got sand

Real quick, can I just say something? It has nothing to do with the story. To be honest, it doesn't have much to do with anything at all. But I just need to get it off my chest. Like, I *literally* need to get it off my chest, my back, my hair, and from inside my shoes.

SAND KIND OF SUCKS.

I just don't get it. Where did billions of tiny rocks even come from? Did a ginormous rock just explode one day, raining its itsy bits around the world? Or did every ant that ever existed just decide to buy a pet rock for themselves, before realizing it was just a boring scam? Either way, these microscopic fragments of rock need to stop being so annoying.

I went to the beach three years ago and I *still* have sand in my shoes. I've had friendships that haven't even lasted that long. Imagine going to

 the beach the day you were born, and then on your 3rd birthday you take off your shoe and see some more sand come out of it. That sounds like a horrible birthday!

All I'm saying is that if I *happened* to meet a genie someday and he *happened* to ask me if I wanted three wishes . . . I would wish for the following:

1. NO MORE SAND!

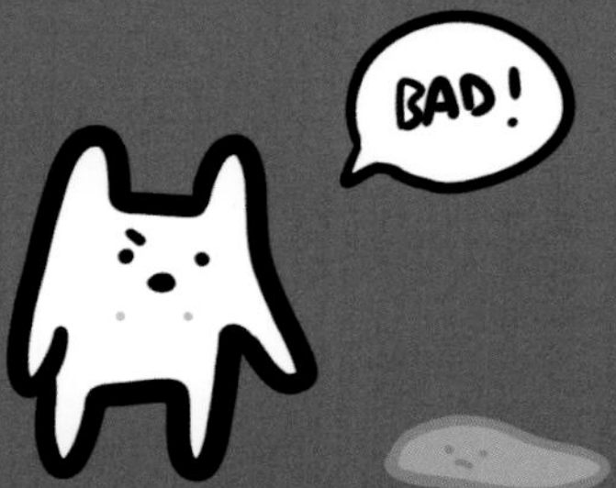
BAD!

2. ICE CREAM THAT NEVER MELTS!

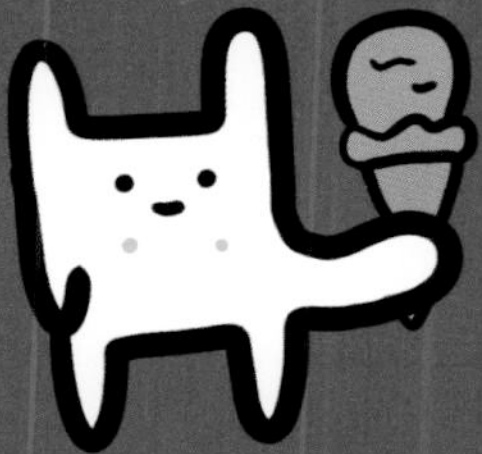

3. A PERFECT SOCIETY WHERE THERE IS NO WAR AND VALUABLE LIFE LESSONS THAT HONE IN ON YOUR CRITICAL THINKING AND CREATIVITY ARE TAUGHT FROM A YOUNG AGE SO THAT EVERY INDIVIDUAL GROWS UP WITH THE NECESSARY TOOLS TO IDENTIFY THEIR SELF-WORTH AND PURPOSE ON THIS NEW PLANET WHERE EVERYONE IS KIND TO EACH OTHER AND LOVE IS ENDLESS.

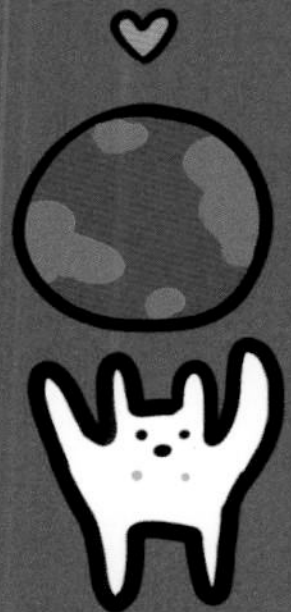

4. A PET MONKEY

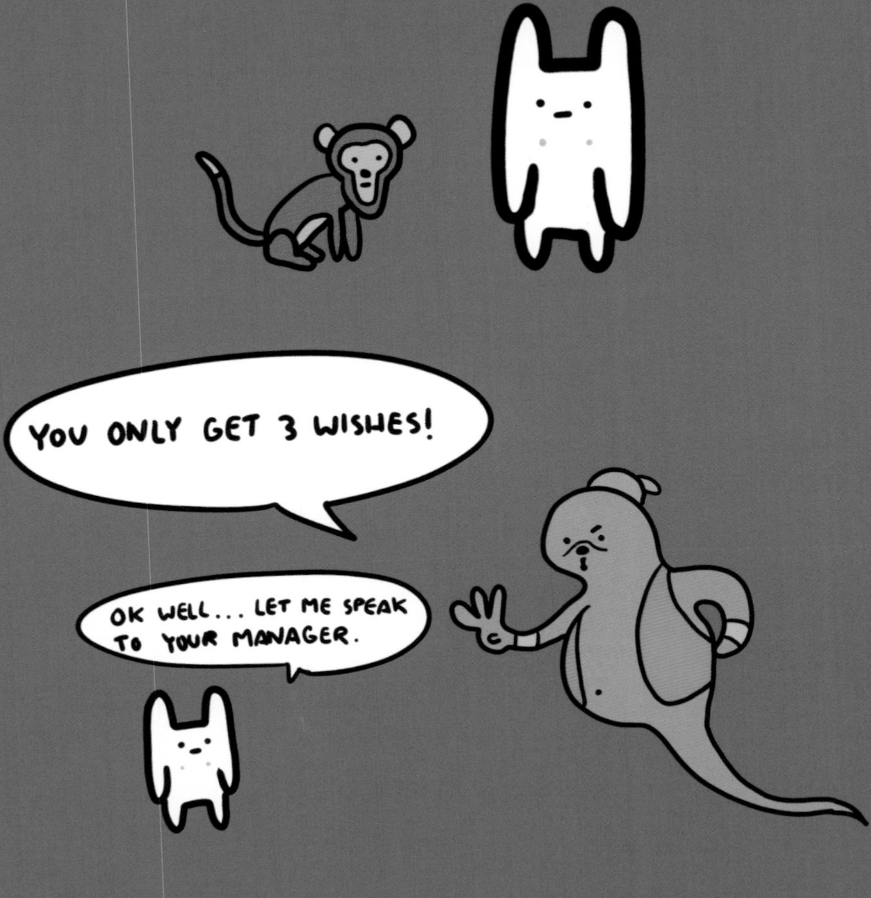
YOU ONLY GET 3 WISHES!
OK WELL... LET ME SPEAK TO YOUR MANAGER.

chapter 7
ur kind (even if others aren't)

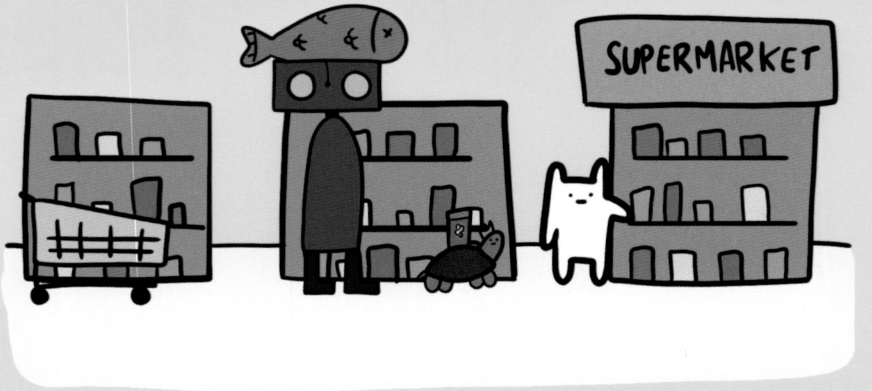
SUPERMARKET

Making sure you treat yourself every now and then is super important. You work hard to do your absolute best in life, and you do a great job. Although it's wise to make sure you eat well and stay on top of your schedule, rewarding yourself for doing so has a time and place too! If all you're doing is working hard, you won't be able to enjoy the little things in life, like seeing movies and eating snacks with friends!

Hm. I can never decide between chunky peanut butter and creamy peanut butter . . .

Why are you even looking at peanut butter? We're supposed to be buying snacks for the movie.

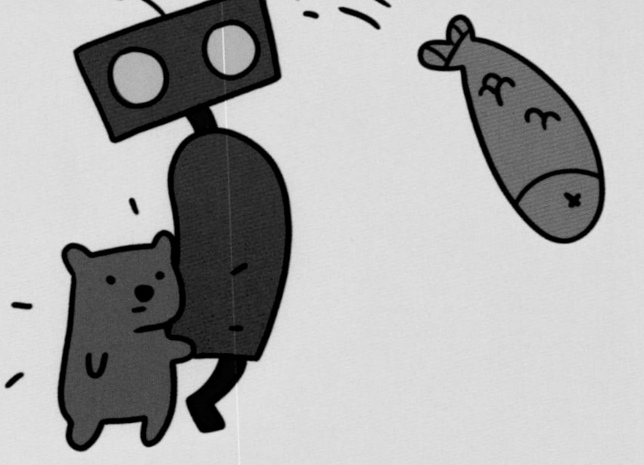

Yeah. *That's what I'm doing*.

My fish!

Hey, why didn't they say "excuse me"? They just bumped right into you!

 That does seem a bit rude. But let's not jump to any conclusions. Maybe we can find out what's going on here . . .

 Hey, uh. You just bumped into my friend and made him drop his expensive salmon. You didn't say anything, which came off a bit rude. We just wanted to make sure everything is all right.

 You wanna fight, clown?!

 Whoa, whoa. Calm down.

 Oh my. I'm so sorry, I didn't even realize! I have so much on my mind. I just failed a test and it's had me in such a bad mood. I apologize for bumping into you, Mr. Robot, sir. I hope your salmon isn't all gross now.

 Oh, it's fine . . . Sorry you failed your test!

Thanks! Goodbye!

He ended up being a very kind bear.

You're right. It's easy to forget, but everyone is going through something in life. We spend a lot of time thinking about ourselves and our own problems, and when we catch someone being rude or grumpy, we like to assume the worst. But sometimes they are just having a bad day. I know I've been caught off guard while I'm having a bad day . . .

 Yeah, me too. One time an old lady asked me where the bus stop was and I yelled at her for being so dumb. I was just upset because I had a rock in my shoe.

 But you don't wear shoes . . .

Oh yeah. Wow, I really should apologize to her then.

 Yeah, you should. That's actually pretty messed up. But you're catching my point. We have to try to keep in mind that everyone is dealing with their own stuff all the time. Instead of being nasty toward them, we should try to meet them with kindness first. It usually goes a long way.

 What about him? Is he just having a rough day?

NO. I'M JUST A MISERABLE PERSON TO BE AROUND.

Oh.

Even the sourest people have their reasons. We can't control other people, we can only control ourselves. So why not try to be the best we can be?

That's why I bought this fish! I just want him to be free!

I think it's broken.

Oh, you poor thing.

On a completely unrelated note, here are some cool ways to hold the door open for someone!

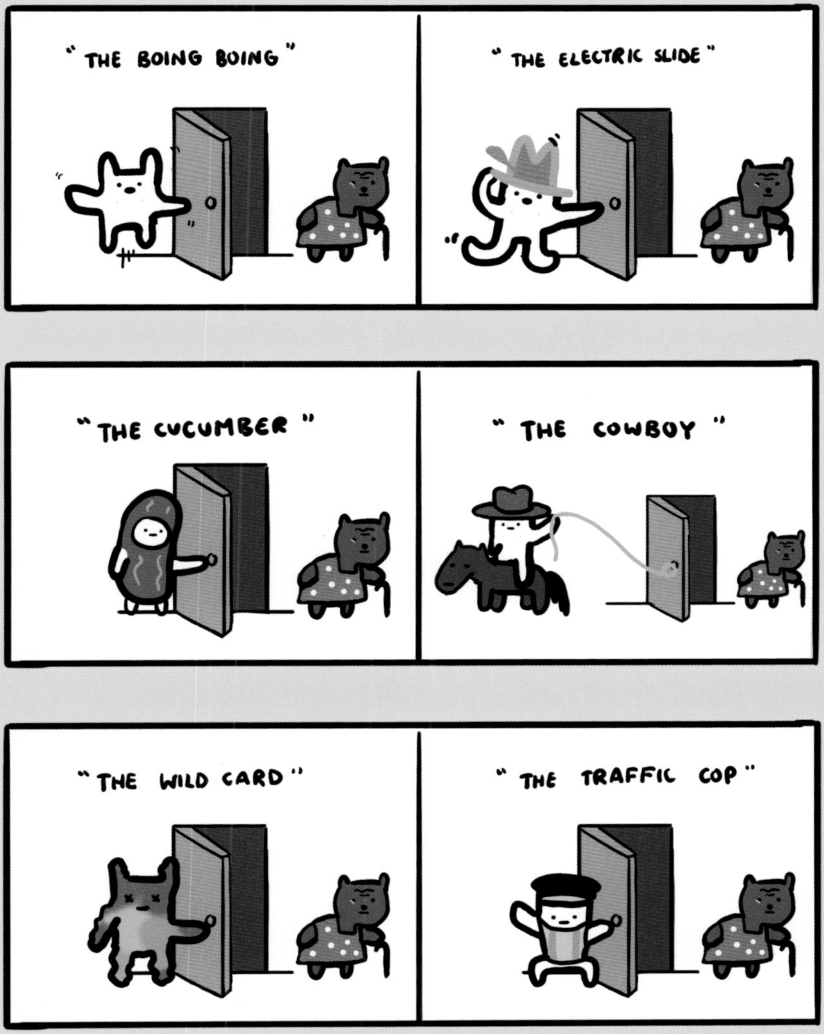
"THE BOING BOING"
"THE ELECTRIC SLIDE"
"THE CUCUMBER"
"THE COWBOY"
"THE WILD CARD"
"THE TRAFFIC COP"

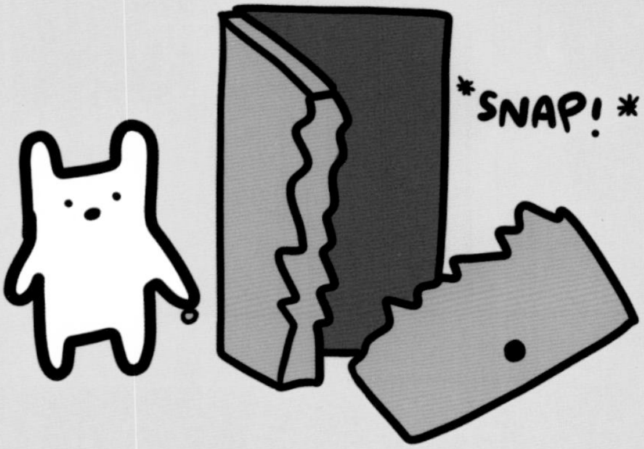
SNAP!

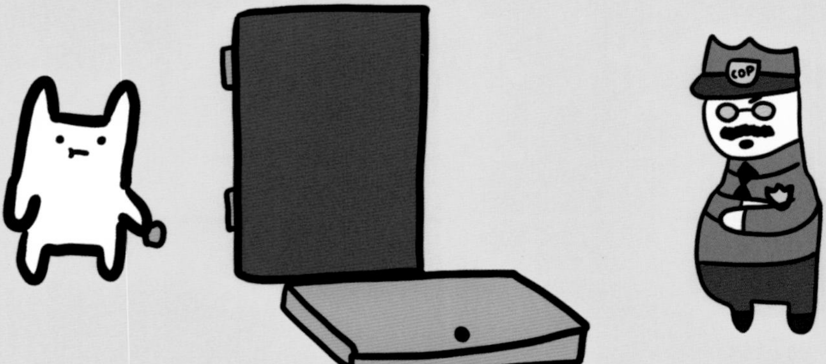
COP

Uh. We should go.

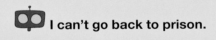 I can't go back to prison.

chapter 8

how r u?

Now that you've learned a few important things, we want to learn some important things about *you*.

WRITE YOUR NAME HERE:

_____

WHAT'S YOUR FAVORITE COLOR?

WOOHOO COLOR ME IN

_____

WHAT'S YOUR FAVORITE ANIMAL?

_____

COMBINE THE LAST 2 TO MAKE AN AWESOME NAME

_____ _____

WHAT WOULD YOU DO DURING A ZOMBIE APOCALYPSE?

_____

LIST **5 THINGS** YOU WANT TO ACCOMPLISH IN YOUR LIFE:

- _____
- _____
- _____
- _____
- _____

DRAW A DOLPHIN PLAYING A SAXOPHONE:

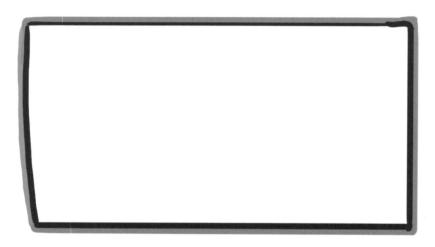

GIVE THEM A NAME:

CONGRATS, YOU JUST LAUNCHED A SEA MAMMAL'S MUSIC CAREER!

QUICKFIRE ROUND CHECKLIST!

- [ ] PICKED A BUG OFF THE SIDEWALK AND PUT IT BACK IN THE GRASS
- [ ] SAID HI TO A NICE STRANGER
- [ ] BEEN TO HAWAII
- [ ] TRIED A NEW FOOD AND LIKED IT
- [ ] HAD A DREAM WHERE YOU WERE FLYING
- [ ] LAUGHED SO HARD YOU STARTED CRYING
- [ ] SAW A PRAYING MANTIS
- [ ] ATE COOKIE DOUGH
- [ ] BOUGHT A GIFT FOR SOMEONE
- [ ] ACCIDENTALLY SAID "YOU TOO" WHEN A WAITER SAYS "ENJOY YOUR MEAL"

- [ ] FELL OFF UR BIKE/ SKATEBOARD
- [ ] TEXTED SOMEONE A MEME
- [ ] SAW A GHOST
- [ ] TRIED A NEW FOOD AND HATED IT
- [ ] PLANTED A FLOWER
- [ ] STAYED AWAKE AT NIGHT
- [ ] BEEN ON A PLANE
- [ ] WON A REALLY HARD VIDEO GAME
- [ ] JUMPED INTO A FREEZING POOL
- [ ] WENT CAMPING

RIP THIS PAGE OUT

$\longrightarrow$

STICK IT ON YOUR WALL

FREE INSPIRATIONAL POSTER

UR DOING

GREAT!

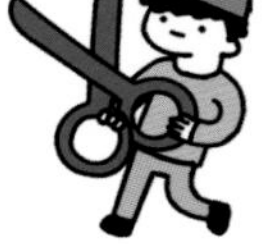

Carefully cut out this page!

DRAW SOME FACES
ON THESE THINGS:

WRITE THE NAMES OF
3 PEOPLE YOU CARE
ABOUT

- _____
- _____
- _____

(IT WILL BRING THEM GOOD LUCK)

FINALLY... CAN YOU SCRATCH MY HEAD?

THANKS.

I FEEL LIKE WE
DEFINITELY BONDED.

chapter 9

ur self

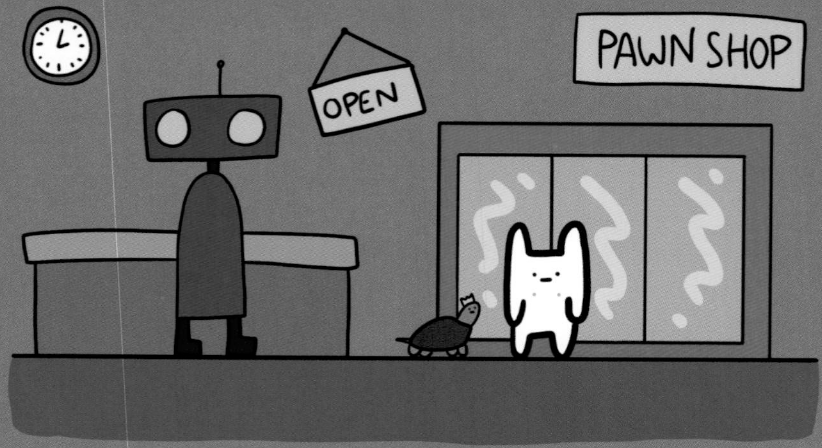
PAWN SHOP
OPEN

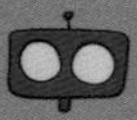
Wow! This store is so cool.

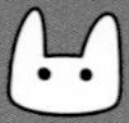
Yeah, it's like they have everything! Exploring new places is one of the most fun and interesting things you could do.

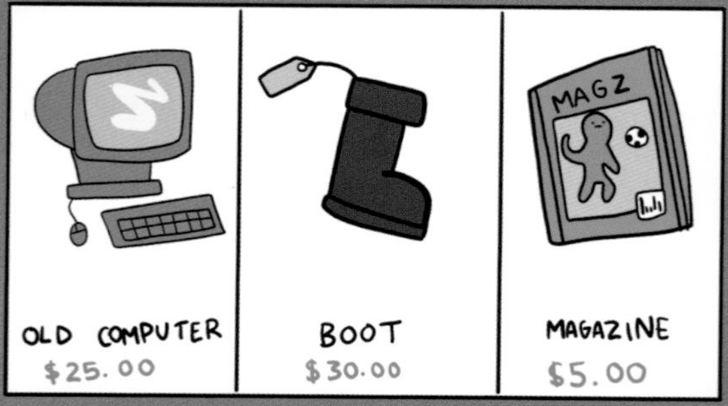
MAGZ
OLD COMPUTER
$25.00
BOOT
$30.00
MAGAZINE
$5.00

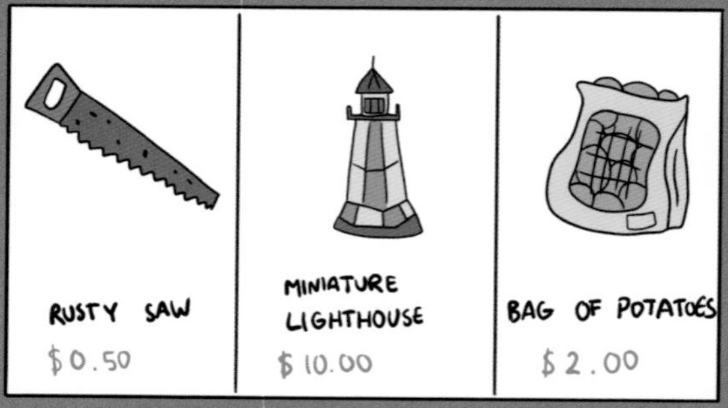
RUSTY SAW
$0.50
MINIATURE LIGHTHOUSE
$10.00
BAG OF POTATOES
$2.00

Even if you think you know your neighborhood like the back of your hand, there are always new places that you never thought of looking into.

One of my favorite things to do is to wander into new shops that I've never been in before. Even if you're not buying anything, oftentimes the shop owners appreciate you walking in and browsing their store. It's a great opportunity to learn more about an area you're in, and a great way to discover something new.

Uh, guys? I think there's something in here . . .

Huh? What do you mean?

I'm a potato.

Whoa! That potato just talked!

Um. Hi, Potato. We are very happy to, uh, meet you?

Hello, Potato, I'm a turtle! I have some self-confidence issues that I'm trying to work on . . . and I wear this crown to cover my bald green scaly head . . .

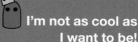 Yeah and I'm . . . uh . . . a robot. I rust easily and I have no arms. I also require motor oil every two weeks. It's actually quite embarrassing.

I don't even know what I am. Am I a cat? A rabbit? What are these dots on my chest?!

I'm not as cool as I want to be!

I don't know how to dance!!

Why am I naked all the time?!

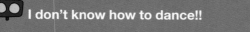 . . . I'm a potato.

Okay . . . but . . . where did you come from? What's your background story?

Did a magical wizard cast a spell on you? Are you actually a handsome prince stuck inside a potato's body?! And the only way you can be changed back to normal is a kiss from your true Turtle-love?!

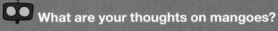

What are your thoughts on mangoes?

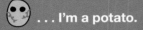

. . . I'm a potato.

Yes. We *know* that.

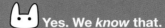

You keep saying the same thing over and over!

Do you want a kiss or not?!

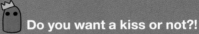

. . . I'm a potato.

No use prying, fellas. That potato is set in his ways. It's beautiful, really.

 But he's not telling us more about himself! He just keeps saying "I'm a potato"! Who is he?

 He knows exactly who he is, and has no desire to prove himself to anyone. We live in a world where everyone is trying to one-up the other. Neighbors fight to have the greener lawn, businesspeople fight to have more money, and people on the Internet fight to have more followers. But not Potato. He is proud of every inch of his starchy self, just the way he is. Sure, he has some issues. A few red spots on his behind, maxed-out credit cards, and an extremely limited vocabulary . . . but that doesn't get him down.

Despite all of the bad that happened to him, he stayed true to himself and stayed his course.

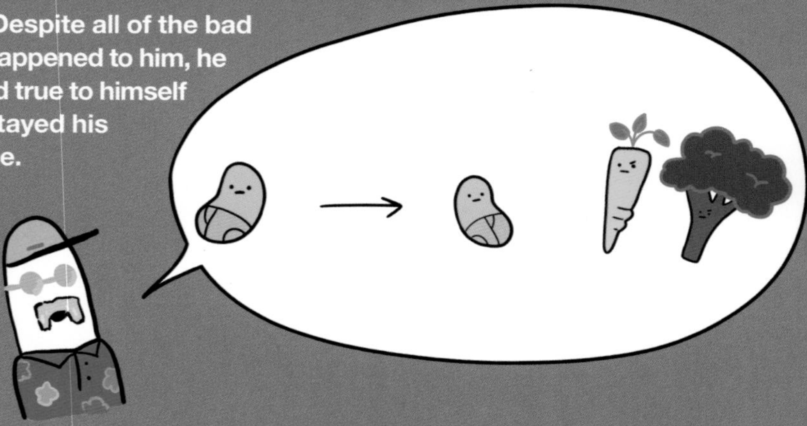

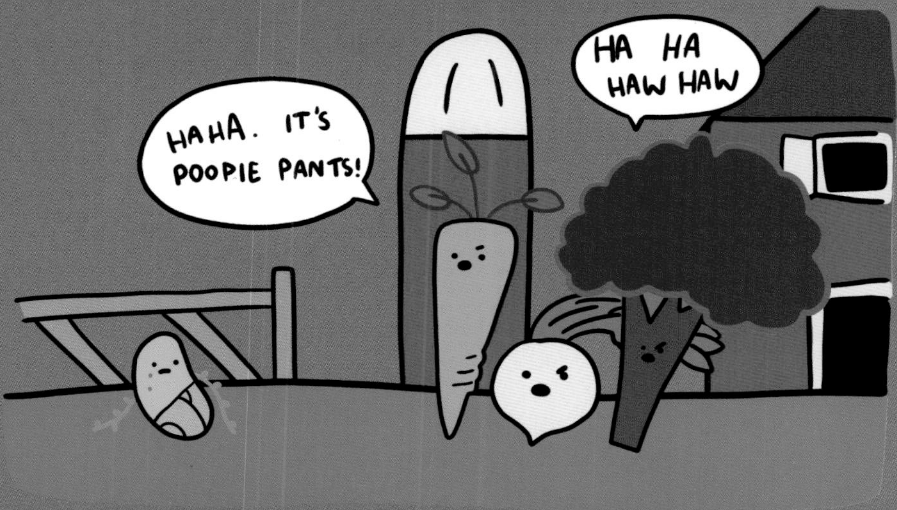
HAHA. IT'S POOPIE PANTS!
HA HA HAW HAW

He wasn't the coolest or most popular vegetable in his neighborhood. But that didn't stop him from graduating at the top of his class and going to a super fancy business school.

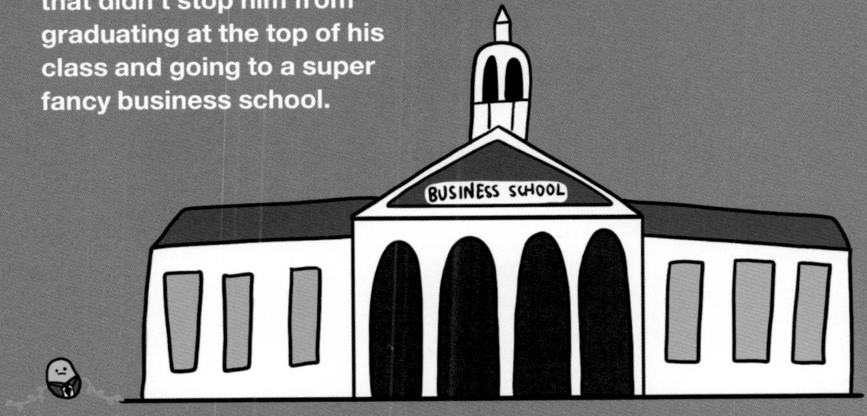
BUSINESS SCHOOL

A few short years later, he was the most successful stock trader in all of New York City. He started his multibillion-dollar company that same year:

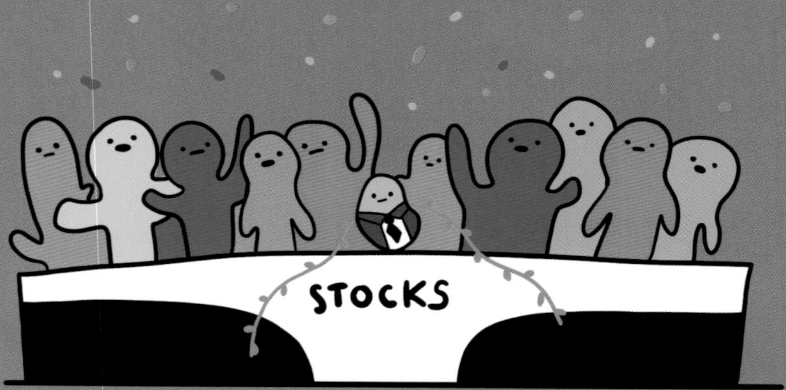
STOCKS

He also starred in a few Hollywood cowboy films along the way.

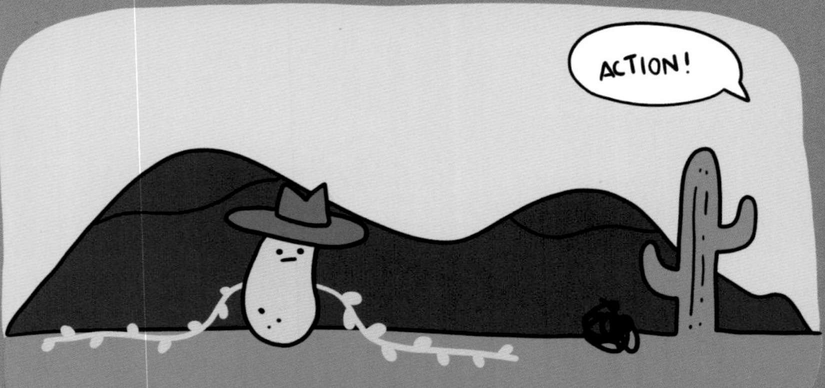
ACTION!

He eventually got so rich and famous that he couldn't leave his house without getting completely bombarded by the paparazzi. He started to feel worn out and depressed, even though he had it all.

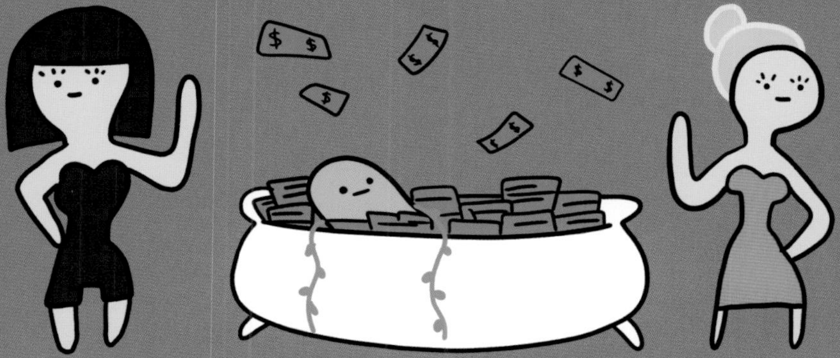

So he left that life behind to travel through the Himalayas with nothing but a backpack and a toothbrush. After spending years up there, searching for life's purpose, he finally achieved true happiness. That's when I met him.

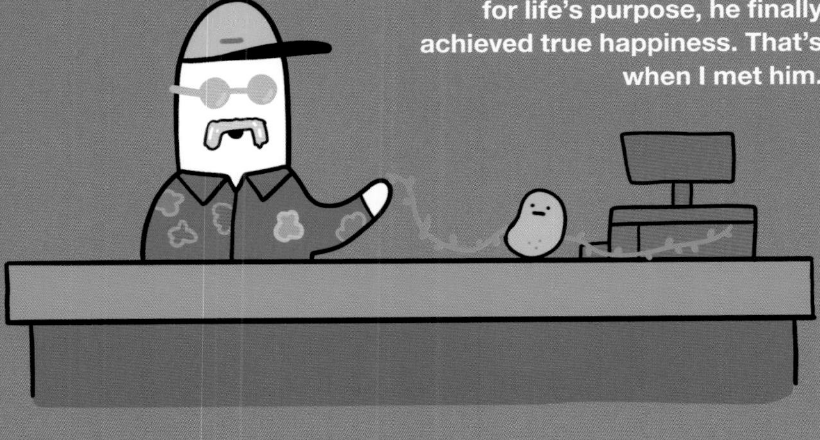

I convinced him it was about time to rest. So here he is, in that old potato sack. All because he learned to love himself. He's the perfect potato. He is proud to be who he is!

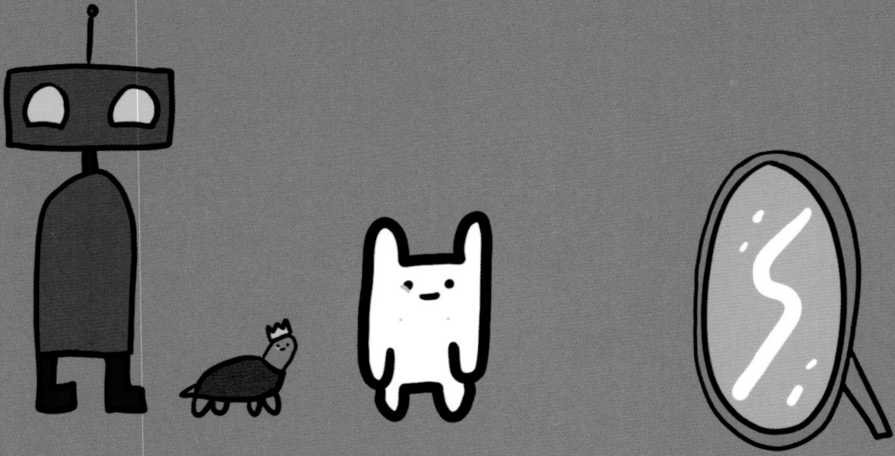

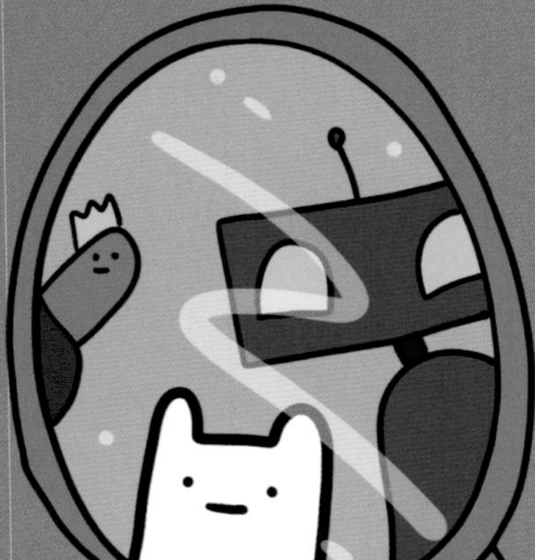

That's . . . beautiful. I am proud to be who I am too!

Me too!

KA-CHING!!

 Me too!
How much can
we buy him for?

Well, that's
just it, fellas. You
can't put a price tag
on self-acceptance.
It's priceless!

Okay, but
seriously. How much?

Seventeen
dollars.

I'M A POTATO!!!

THE PAWN SHOP

chapter 10
u should ask
(if u need to)

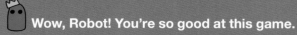

Wow, Robot! You're so good at this game.

Yes, this game helped me overcome my fear of both snakes and cake.

I'm a potato.

99999580
FUN TIME
CHECK IT
RAP FIGHT
SNAKE
FAT BOY

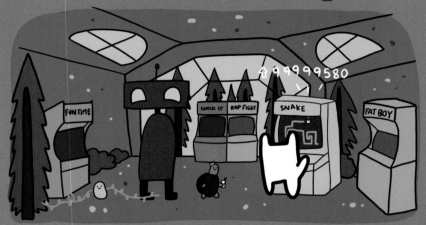

Yeah, it's definitely great hanging out with all of you. New friends can be the best type of friends. There's so much to learn about each other, and every experience is new and exciting! Now I just have to figure out how to get extra movie tickets last minute . . . OH MY—WE FORGOT ABOUT THE MOVIE! Let's get out of here!

Oh my goodness. Cue the disclaimer so parents don't get mad at us!

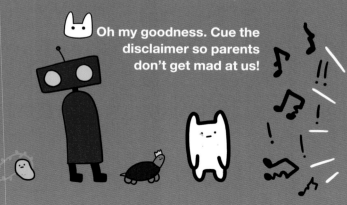

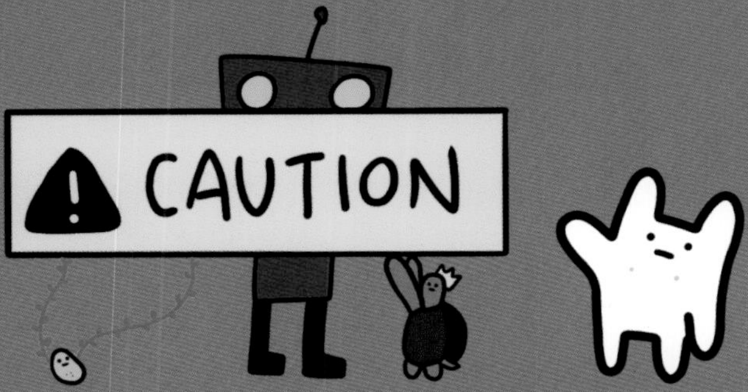
CAUTION

DISCLAIMER:

PLEASE NOTE THAT ANY AND ALL USE OF THE AFOREMENTIONED BIRD WHISTLES IS ENTIRELY AT THE BEHEST OF THE WHISTLER, AND IS IN NO WAY ENCOURAGED OR OTHERWISE ENDORSED BY THE AUTHOR OF THIS BOOK. THE AUTHOR CANNOT BE HELD RESPONSIBLE FOR ANY REPLICATION OF THESE BIRD WHISTLES, ESPECIALLY IF YOU ARE IN CLOSE PROXIMITY TO A TREE, A BUSH, A BIRD HOUSE, A FOREST, A PET STORE, A ZOO, OR LAS VEGAS. PLEASE NOTE THAT THE USE OF THESE WHISTLES WILL LIKELY RESULT IN ARREST OR FINES FOR FOWL PLAY.

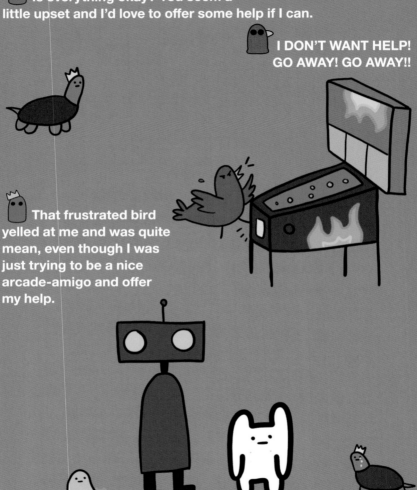

Is everything okay? You seem a little upset and I'd love to offer some help if I can.

I DON'T WANT HELP! GO AWAY! GO AWAY!!

That frustrated bird yelled at me and was quite mean, even though I was just trying to be a nice arcade-amigo and offer my help.

He's obviously a terrible, rotten bird. I guess we should leave so we can make it in time for the movie . . .

Wait, we should stay. Just because that bird yelled at you, saying he doesn't want help, doesn't mean he doesn't *need* it. You offered, which was very nice of you. All too often, those who reject help are the ones who need it most. Maybe, if we just *show* him what help looks like, we can break through his defensive barrier and make him feel so much better.

I actually went to college with that pinball machine. I could probably help.

I'm a potato . . .

Yes, we know, Potato. College *is* very expensive.

Hey. My friend here said that you told her you don't need any assistance, but it's quite clear that you're having some trouble beating this game. The thing is, that game you're playing is actually one of the toughest games in the whole joint! It's okay to ask for help, Mr. Bird. In fact, if we were to work together, we could probably beat this game in no time. There is no need to get upset, because there are people out there who can help you!

HEY, NANCY, LONG TIME NO TALK! I SAT BEHIND YOU IN SCIENCE CLASS.
OMG, HEY ROB!

 Life is hard, Mr. Bird. It's full of road bumps and obstacles. Heck, sometimes even I get overwhelmed and frustrated, and the last thing I want to do is talk to someone. But what I realized is . . . sometimes you can't do it all by yourself. And that's perfectly okay!

 You *shouldn't* have to do it all by yourself. There are people out there who love and care about you who would be happy to help.

 And in the end, you'll be glad that you did get that help. Because it makes things more fun and worthwhile along the way. Life doesn't need to be harder than it is!

 We are here for you, Mr. Bird!

NEW HI-SCORE
1. BIRD_   9999999
2. LIL BEAR   9999980
3. OFFICER   9999900
4. SHOP OWNER   9980750

HOORAY!!

Wow, thanks, everyone. Sometimes I get too buried in my own negative thoughts to see the positive people in my life. I appreciate you showing me how much easier life can be, with just a little help from friends and family. Want the rest of my taco?

I'd love to have it, thanks!

Glad we could help. But I guess we can't go to the movies after all. It's way too late now—we won't make it over there in time . . .

What do you mean? There's a bus stop right around the corner from here! If we leave now, we can all catch it!

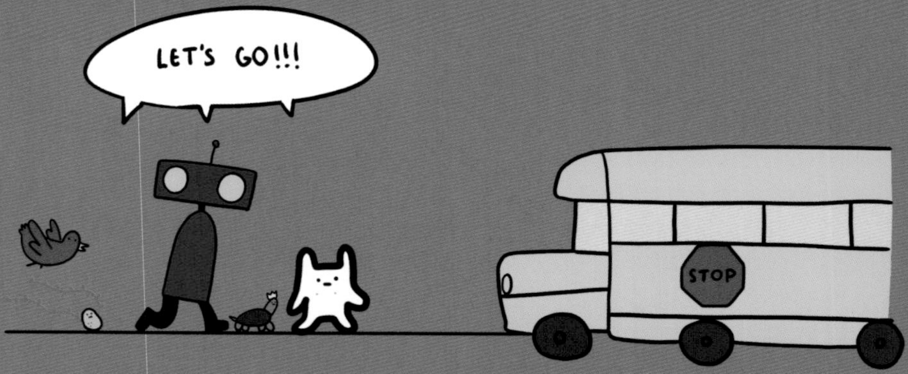
LET'S GO!!!
STOP

chapter 11
u ever think about slugs?

Yo, do you ever think about slugs?
I think about them all the time.

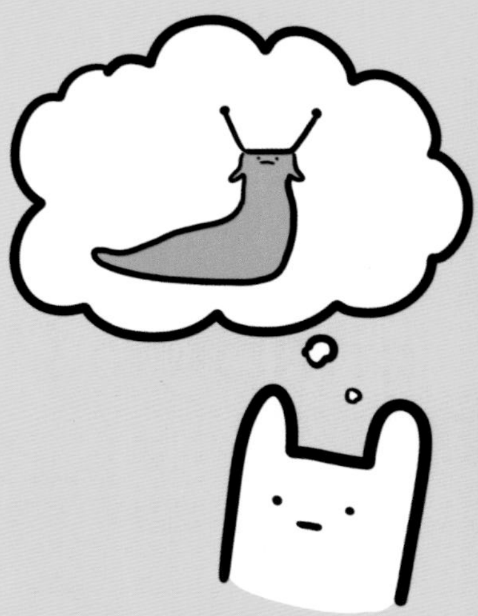

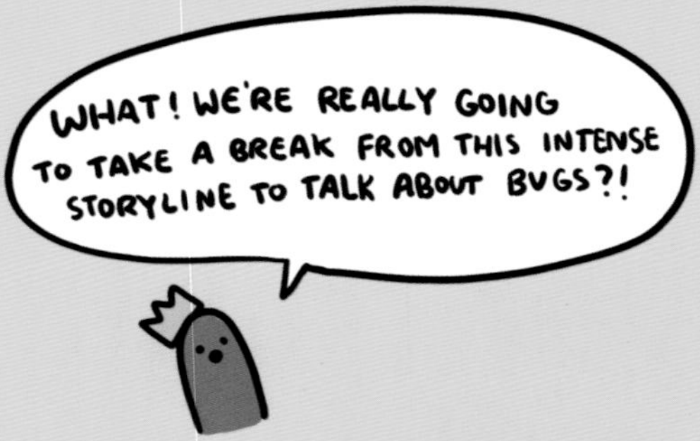
WHAT! WE'RE REALLY GOING TO TAKE A BREAK FROM THIS INTENSE STORYLINE TO TALK ABOUT BUGS?!

No, not bugs. *Slugs*. I mean, they are freaks of nature! Long dangly eyes, a squishy body, and oozy slime! If they were giant, they would be literal monsters straight out of a horror movie!

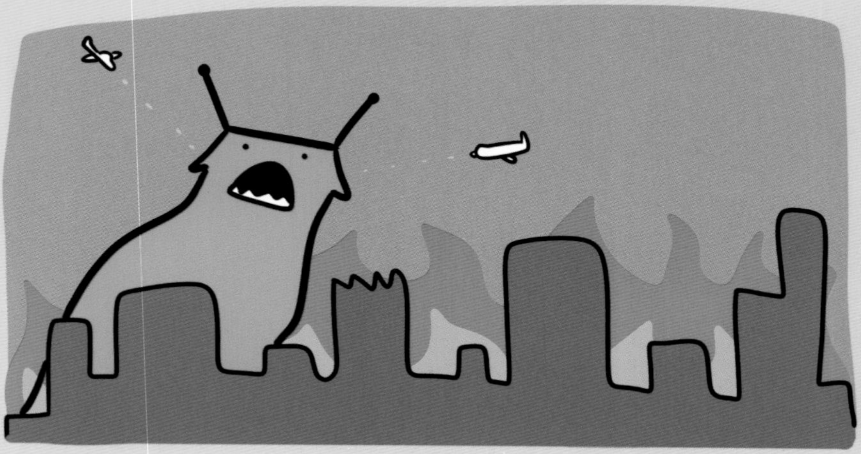

But they are small and tiny. And you know what else? I honestly feel like they might be misunderstood. Maybe they have incredible personalities. My mom always taught me not to judge a book by its cover, even if the book cover is gross and disturbing! I just wish I could speak to a slug to find out.

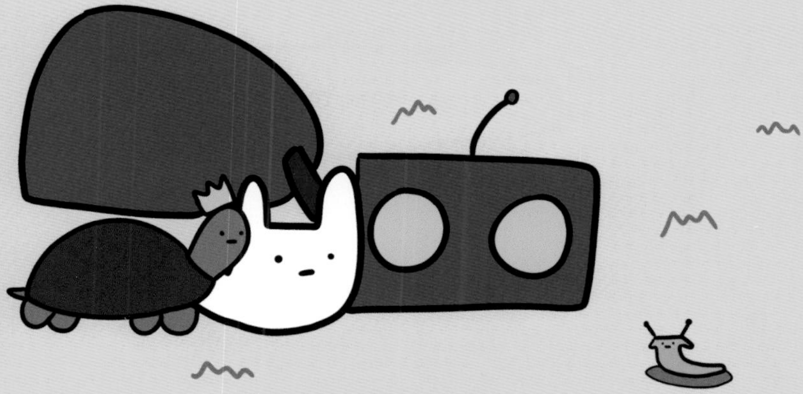

Incredibly enough, slugs have been around for 150 million years. That's more prehistoric than the Tyrannosaurus rex! Maybe at one point in time, a T. rex and a slug became best friends.

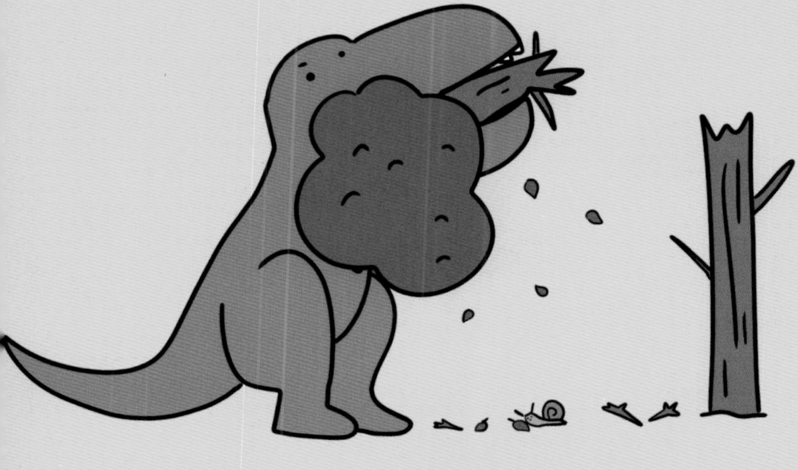

After all, I'm sure the two very different creatures could learn a lot from each other. Maybe the slug even helped with dino-dating. Now, that would be nice of him.

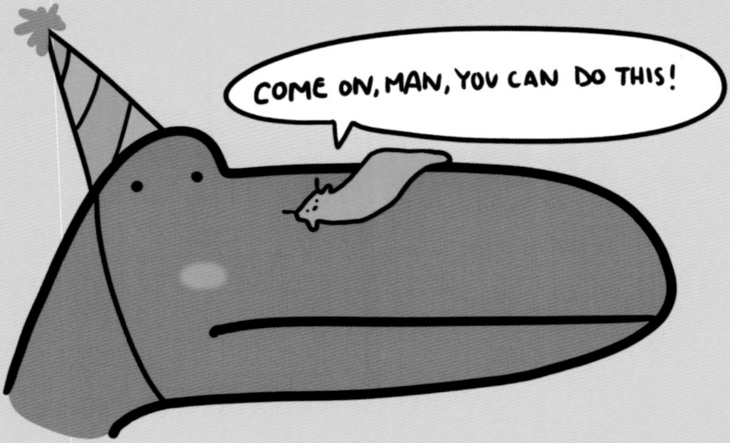
COME ON, MAN, YOU CAN DO THIS!

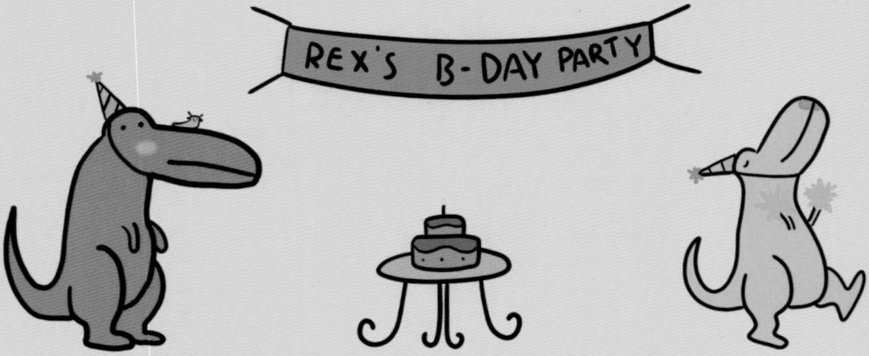
REX'S B-DAY PARTY

I'm not sure why slugs have been around for so long. I'm also not sure what role they play in mother nature. Maybe their slime acts as a nice tasty glaze for other bugs to eat and enjoy. Or maybe their eyes can see into the past and the future at the same exact time.

Either way, I think slugs are pretty cool and stuff.

That's it. That's all this chapter was about.

Moving on.

chapter 12

ur sad

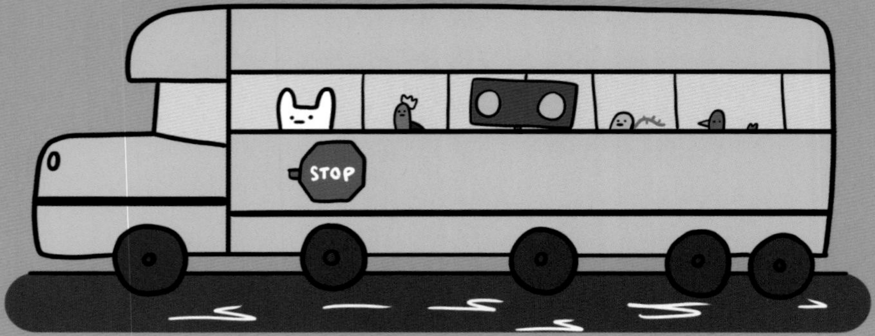
STOP

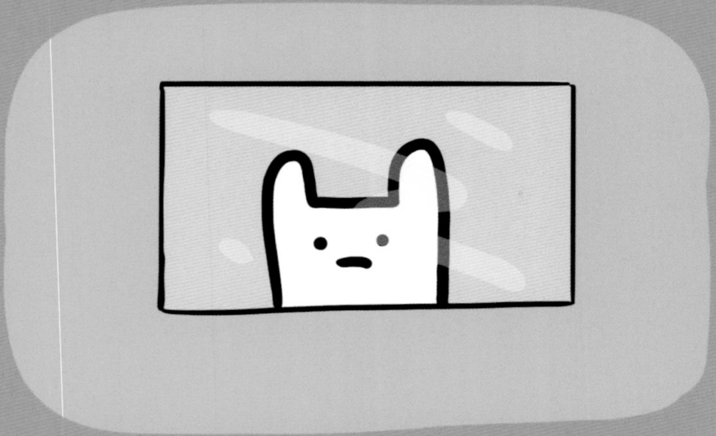

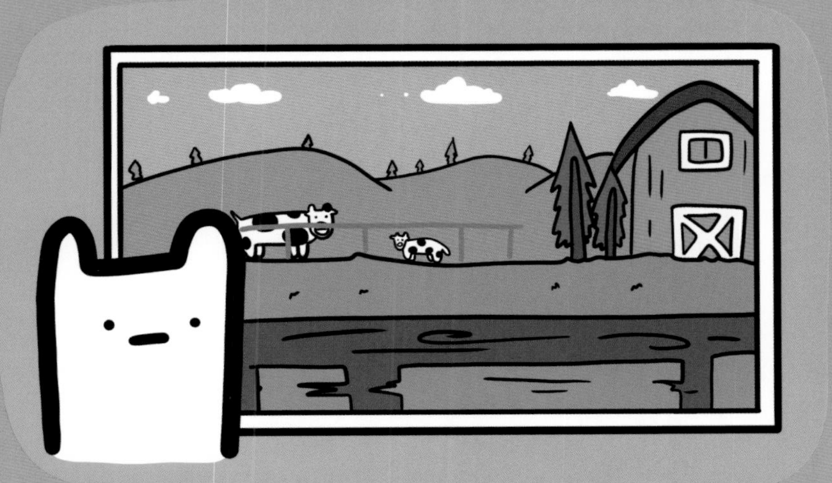

Hey, what's wrong? Aren't you excited for the movie?

Yeah, but I'm afraid we might miss it. The bus is going so slow . . . Who's driving this thing?

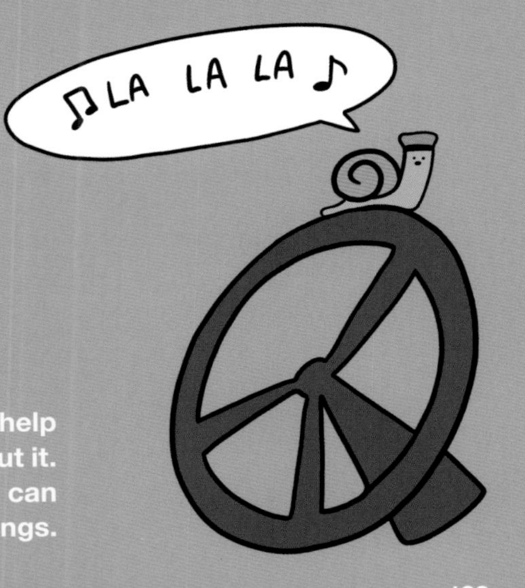
♫ LA LA LA ♪

Ah, we'll be fine. We're gonna make it! Don't worry about it.

I can't help *but* worry about it. On certain days, all I can do is worry about things.

I get anxious and upset for no reason, and I wish that it would all just go away. I fantasize about a version of myself that isn't like this. But this feeling creeps up on me and I have a hard time getting rid of it sometimes.

I know the exact feeling you're talking about. Some days I wake up and feel tired right away, like the world is trying to pull me down. I always try to do the things that make me happy and energized, and sometimes they work. But on the days when they don't work, it spooks me into thinking that there's something really wrong with me.

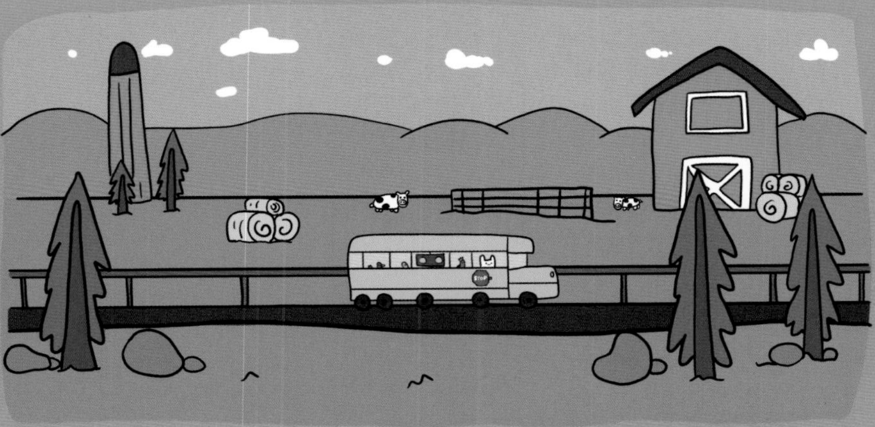

I can relate to this. I take many naps on days like this, hoping that when I wake up, all these feelings will have disappeared. But they are usually still there. I even try cleaning my hard drive or tightening my screws, but even that rarely helps when I'm feeling down.

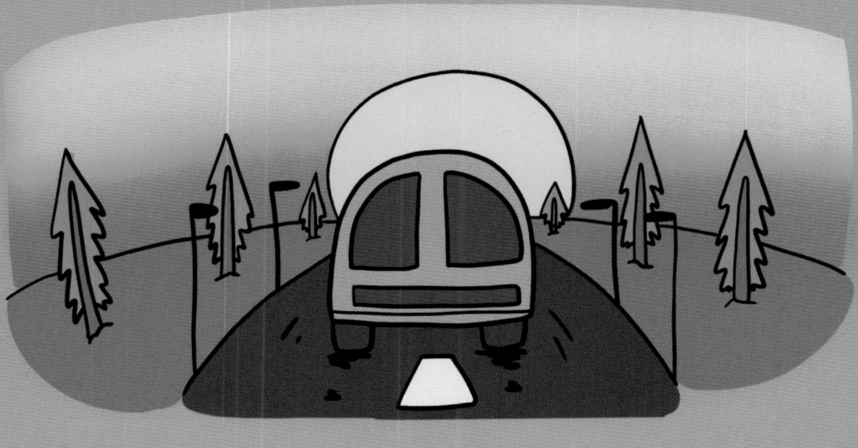

Man, you guys really are speaking my language here. I can't tell you how many days I've spent just cooped up in my birdhouse, eating way too many bird seeds, bummed that my life isn't way cooler and exciting. I try to tell myself that tomorrow will be different. Sometimes it is, sometimes it isn't.

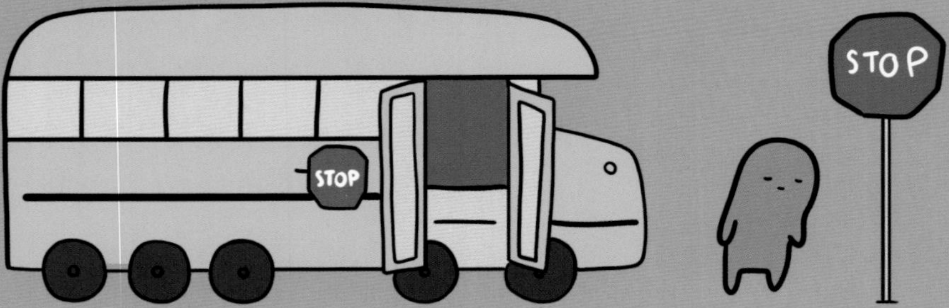
STOP
STOP

I'm a potato.

I wish there was a book for this too, Potato.

Whoa! Hey! Sir! You forgot this!

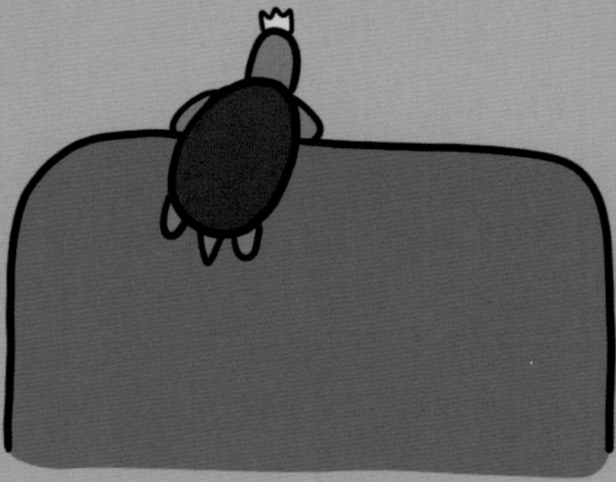

Aw man, that blue dude just left without his book!

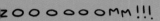

ZOOOOOOMM!!!

What is it? It looks pretty cool.

**Should we open it?
It's not illegal to open
someone else's book . . . is it?**

**No, I don't think so.
But want to see a list of
things that are *actually* illegal?**

127

THINGS THAT ARE ACTUALLY ILLEGAL

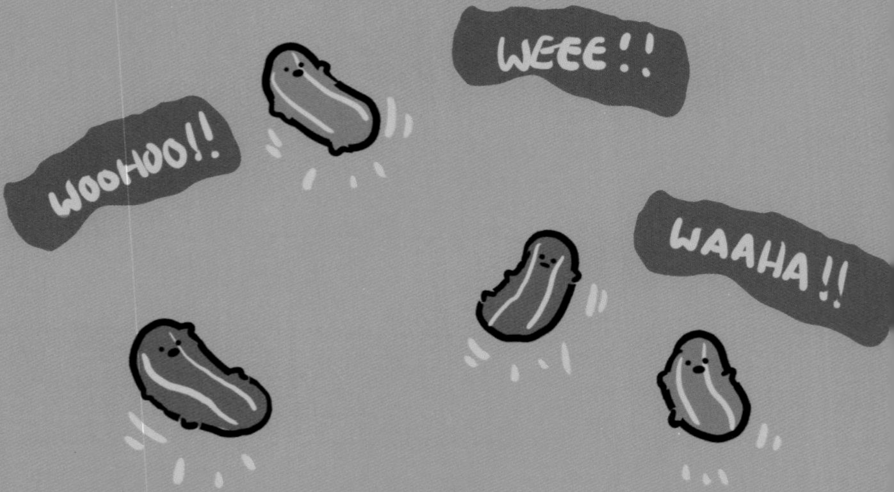
WEEE!!
WOOHOO!!
WAAHA!!

CONNECTICUT: PICKLES MUST BOUNCE

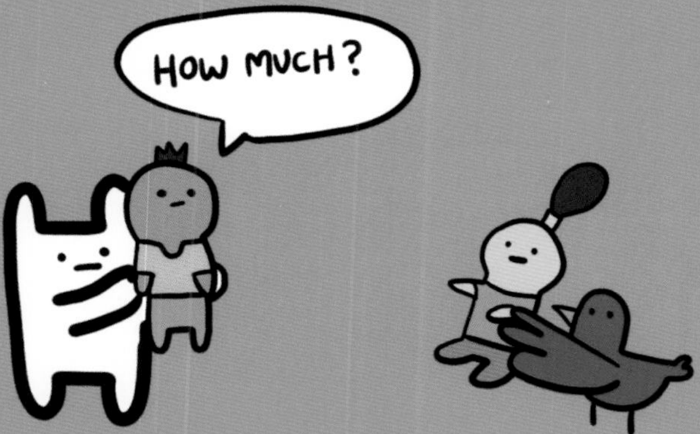
HOW MUCH?

FLORIDA: NO SELLING CHILDREN

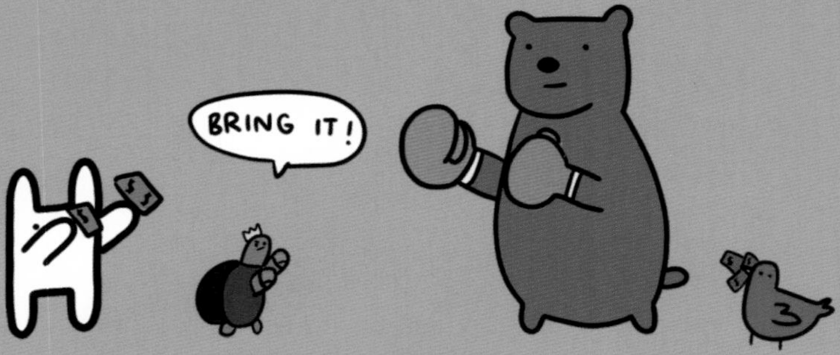
BRING IT!

OKLAHOMA: NO BEAR WRESTLING

WASHINGTON: NO SASQUATCH POACHING

NEW HAMPSHIRE: NO SEAWEED COLLECTING

 WHOA!!!

Who are you?

I am the Knower of
All Secrets. Some say I'm only a myth.
Some say a legend. But alas,
here I am, to tell you all some
tales in this time of need.

 Knower of all secrets?
Prove it.

Well, for one,
I know that you really want
to eat me right now.

Yeah, well, that's
obvious. I skipped lunch
today and you look delicious.

 I also know that several years ago you
tried to build the coolest sandcastle
on the beach. You were almost done with
this masterpiece of sand that would've
definitely impressed the bird you were in love with,
who was accompanying you that day, but
a bully named Samuel came over and stomped
on it until your cool sandcastle was no more.
You ran all the way home in your flip-flops, crying.

Oh . . . uh . . . I forgot about that.

Ooh! Do me! Do me!

Hmm . . . it seems that one day last year you got
so bored that you stuck your antenna into a beehive just to see
what it felt like. You went to the hospital shortly after. Weird.

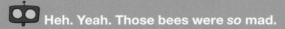 Heh. Yeah. Those bees were *so* mad.

Okay, so, this is super embarrassing.

 Can we just read your book?

But of course! As long as you are mentally prepared to handle the secrets that lie within. The secrets . . . to achieve complete and total HAPPINESS!

 Go ahead, man, open it!

 Okay, here I go . . .

THINGS TO REMEMBER WHEN
UR SAD*
* OR JUST NOT ENTIRELY VERY HAPPY :-
BY WORMY WORM

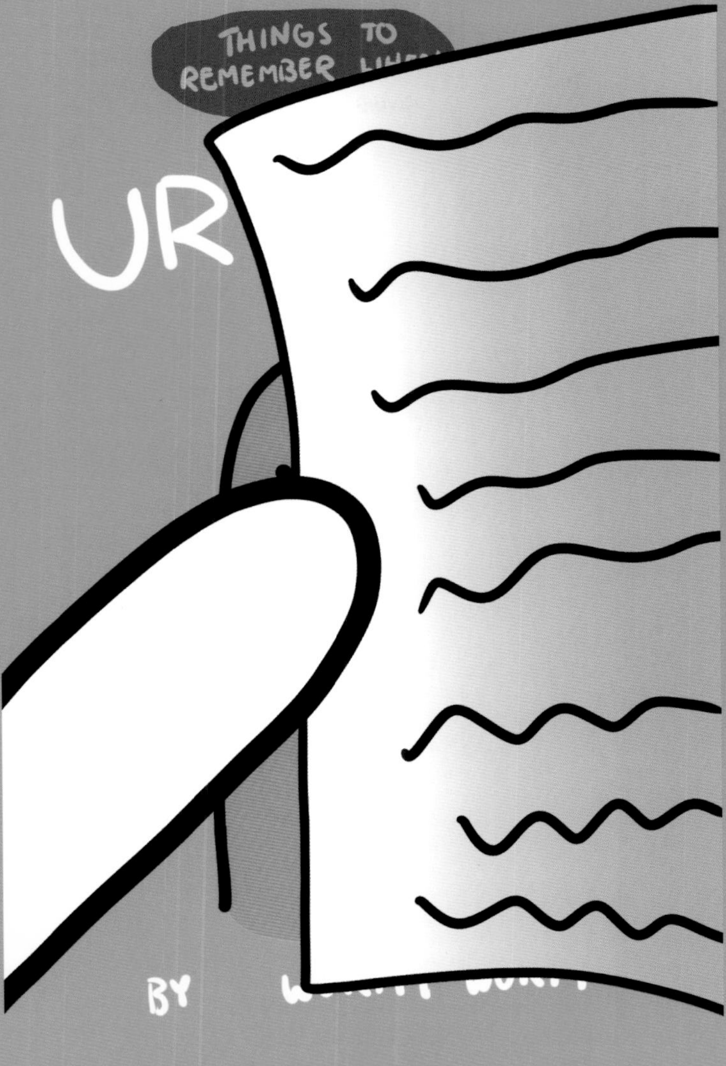
THINGS TO
REMEMBER
UR
BY

DOG IN SUNGLASSES

SMELL OF RAIN

WALKS AT NIGHT

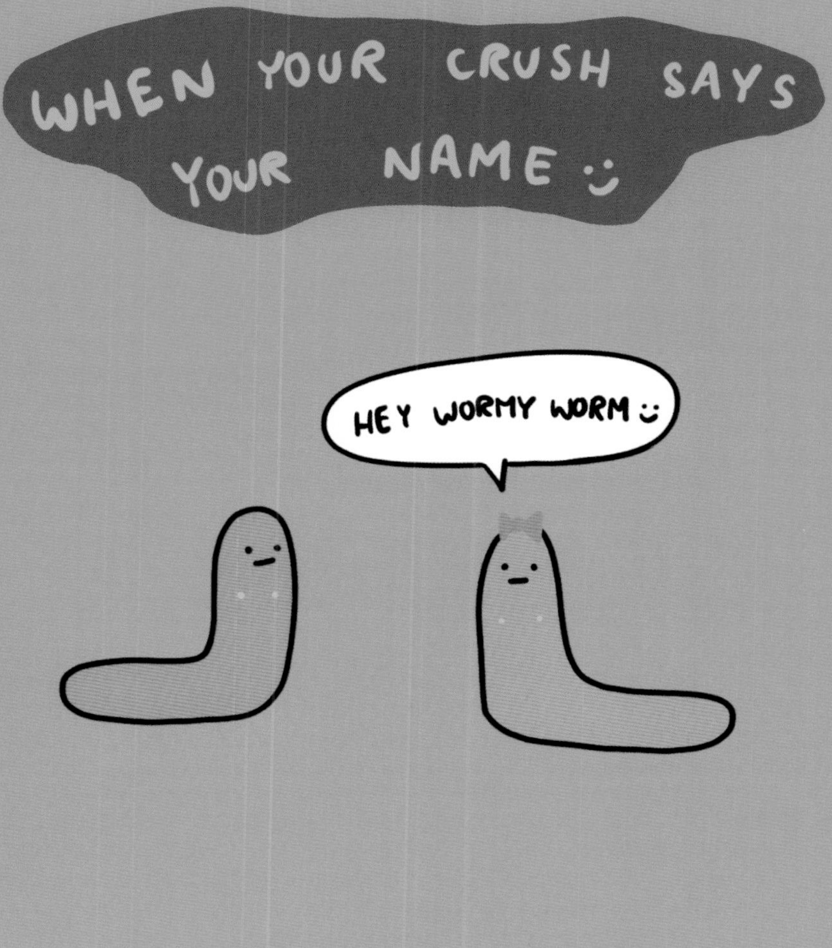
WHEN YOUR CRUSH SAYS YOUR NAME :)
HEY WORMY WORM :)

BAKERIES

TASTEE · BAKERY

SMILING BABIES

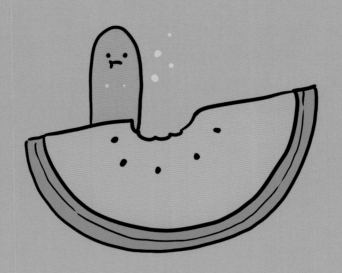

TASTE OF WATERMELON
IN THE SUMMERTIME

HANGING OUT WITH FRIENDS

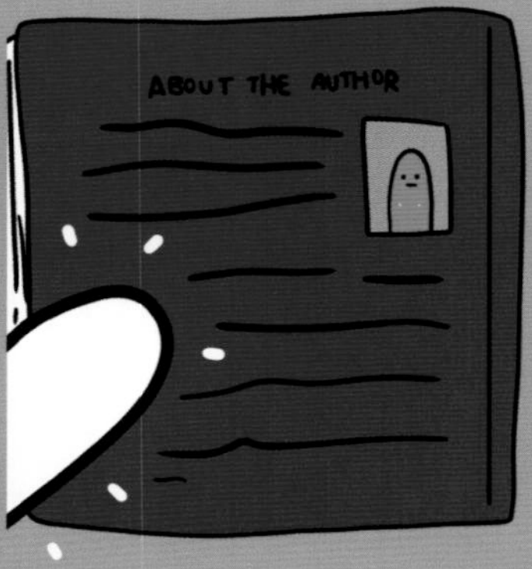
ABOUT THE AUTHOR

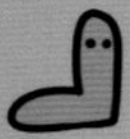

As you can see, there are so many reasons to be happy. Even though that rotten feeling may pop up into your head every once in a while, it's important to keep these things in mind to remind yourself that all in all, things are not so bad. The simple pleasures in life are always there for you.

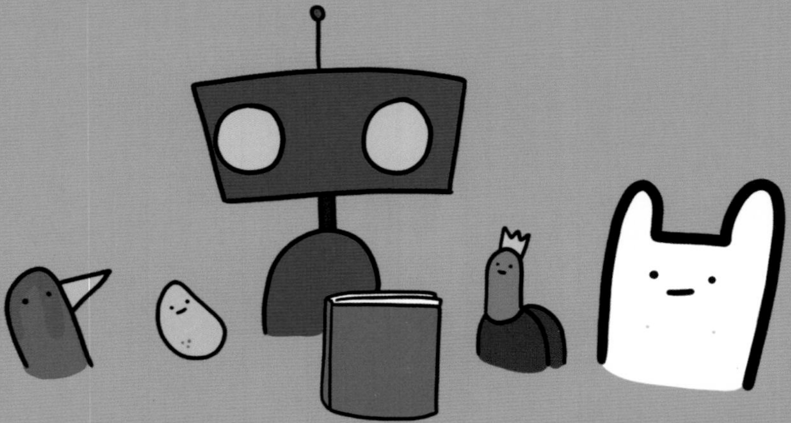

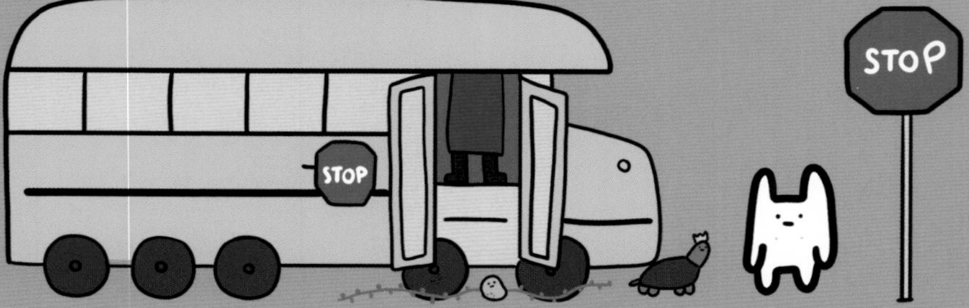
STOP
STOP

Thanks, Knower of All Secrets. We feel much better now.

 Hey, thanks for finding my book, friend! Pretty good read, right?

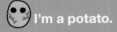 Oh yeah, no problem. How did you catch up with us, though?

 I ran. Like, really fast.

 I'm a potato.

 Come on, everyone! The movie is almost starting!

 Cool!

147

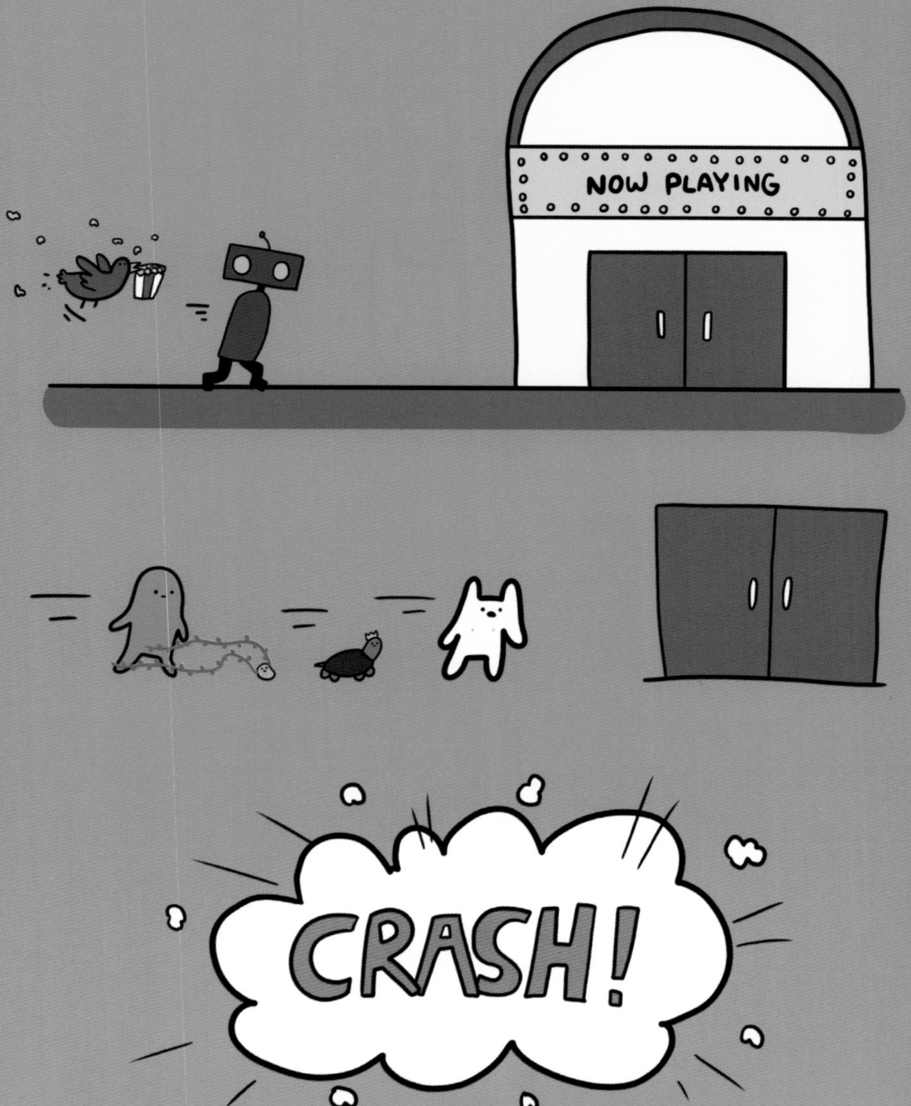
NOW PLAYING
CRASH!

WHAT'S A MOOOOOVIE?
NOW PLAYING

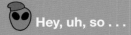

Hey, uh, so . . .

OKAY, FINE, JUST JOIN US!

chapter 13

making ur
new friends

 Even if your new friends try to sabotage your moviegoing experience, they're still really great to have. There are plenty of ways to make a new friend. It's important to meet new people because they spice up your life in ways you never thought was even possible!

MEETING NEW PEOPLE:

PROS : NEW ADVENTURES

PROS: NEW IDEAS

WHHHOOOAAA!!!

PROS : MORE INSPIRATION

LOOKS LIKE I'M OUT OF ROLLS
I GOTCHU, MAN

PROS : EXTRA HELP

PROS : INCREASED SMILES

SO... WHAT'S UR FAVORITE SANDWICH?
YE.

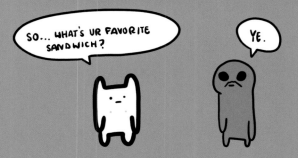

CONS : SOMETIMES THEY TURN OUT TO BE A LITTLE WEIRD, BUT WHO CARES.

It can be a little nerve-wracking to meet new people, but I've created an easy step-by-step guide to make it as easy as possible!

STEP 1: INTRODUCE YOURSELF

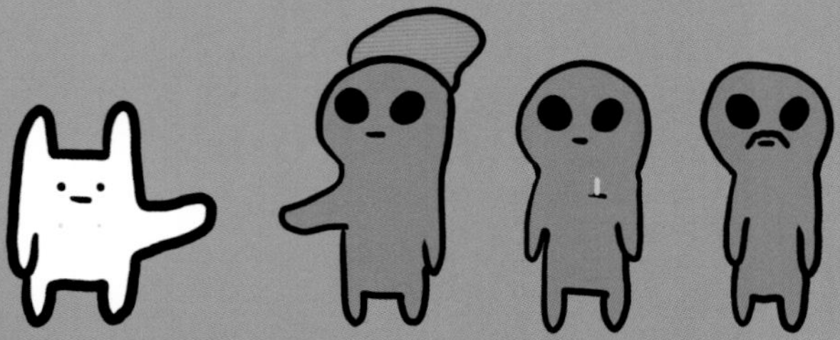

STEP 2: LEARN ABOUT THEIR NAME AND OTHER THINGS

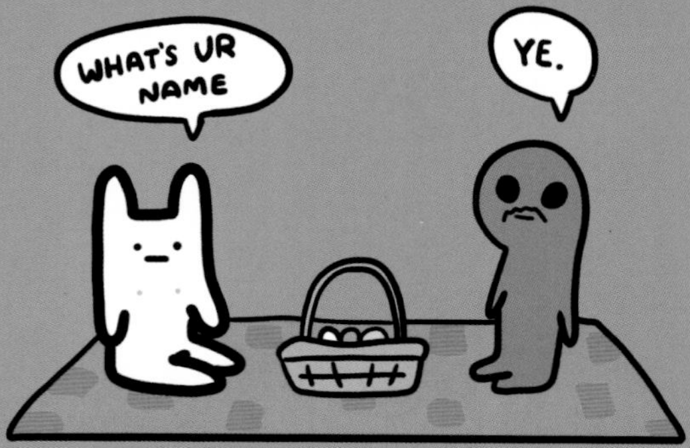
WHAT'S UR NAME
YE.

STEP 3: ASK ABOUT DIETARY RESTRICTIONS

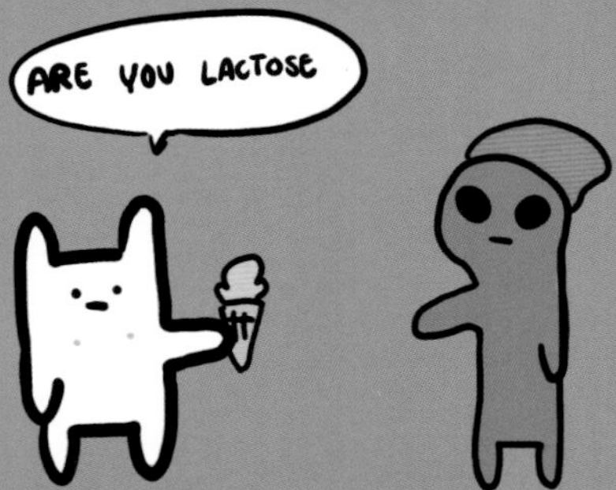
ARE YOU LACTOSE

STEP 4: GO ON A FUN ADVENTURE. IT CAN BE A SUPER CRAZY ONE, OR JUST HANG IN YOUR BASEMENT.

 Having a good friend is like having a pocket of love and inspiration in your life. It's a beautiful thing and it works both ways!

STEP 5: LEARN FROM EACH OTHER, SHARE WITH EACH OTHER, CARE FOR EACH OTHER!

Sometimes, two friends aren't alike. And that's okay! Friends can be different from each other. In fact, it's great to have many different friends to pair with your many different interests and hobbies.

Sometimes it might be awkward to introduce them to each other . . .

KIND

DETERMINED

CALM

CARING

WISE

GENTLE

But as long as you enjoy yourself when you're with them, that's all that matters!

 Overall, having a friend group that consists of different qualities and backgrounds helps make *you* a better person. They offer new perspectives, new stories, and can even teach you new things. Having a bunch of different friends is the way to go!

YAY DIVERSITY!

chapter 14
ur human!

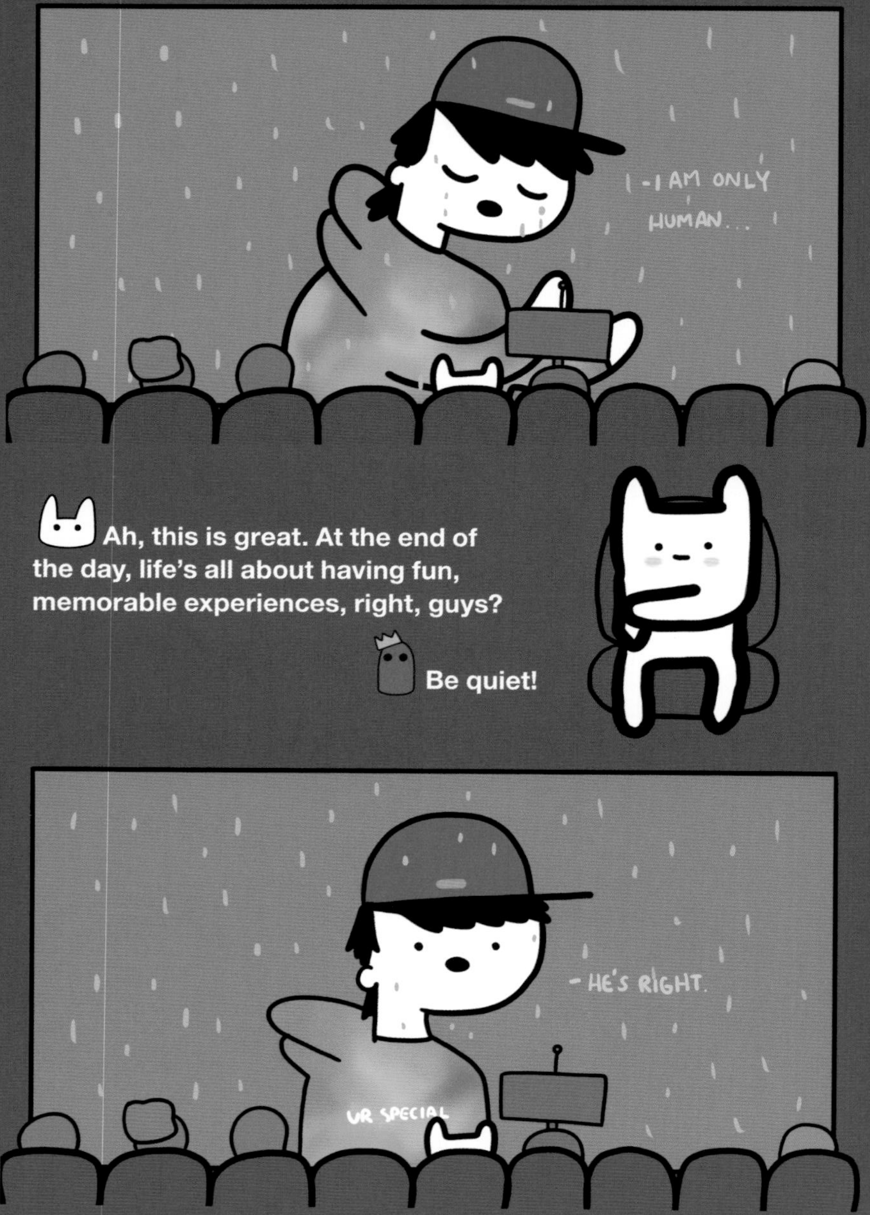
I-I AM ONLY HUMAN...
Ah, this is great. At the end of the day, life's all about having fun, memorable experiences, right, guys?
Be quiet!
-HE'S RIGHT.
UR SPECIAL

Who are you?

I'm the main character of this book!

Uh, *excuse me*?
How can *you* be the
main character?! You only
showed up at the end!

Yeah, well, I'm the author of this book. Look, my name on my driver's license matches the name on the front cover!

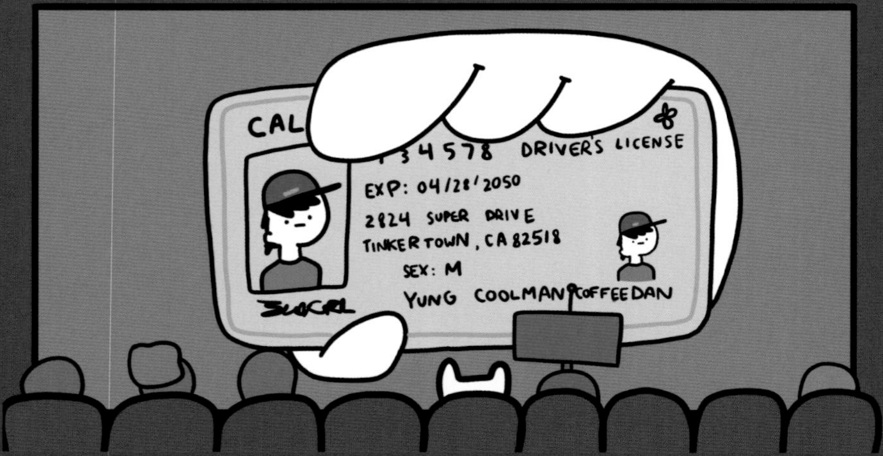
CAL
DRIVER'S LICENSE
EXP: 04/28/2050
2824 SUPER DRIVE
TINKERTOWN, CA 82518
SEX: M
YUNG COOLMAN COFFEEDAN

Ewwwwww!

Gross!

You really need to have that updated . . . you look *horrible!*

Look, everyone. Let me be real with you. The readers of this book are all going to be humans like me, and maybe one or two well-trained gorillas. That's it. No cute little naked cat-things, no turtles, and definitely no potatoes.

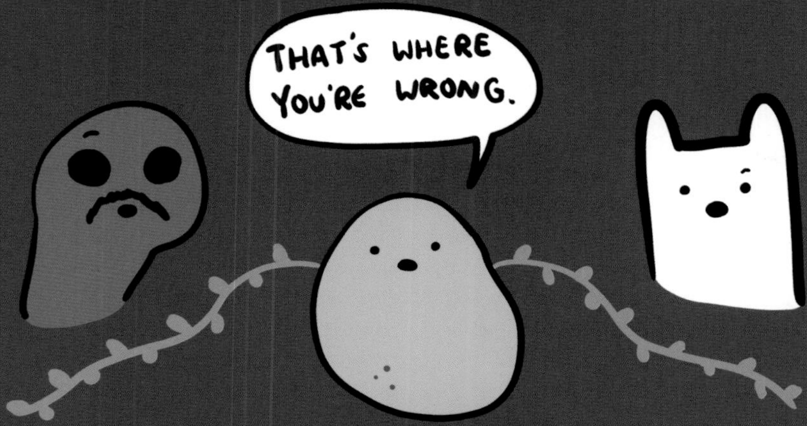
THAT'S WHERE YOU'RE WRONG.

Wait, did you just say something new?

Erm . . . I'm a potato.

Uh.

Not to say they don't love you cute little creatures. You actually helped them remember a few important things. Like how to love yourself and gain self-confidence. Or how important it is to cherish the memories you have with someone. And even how to make a new friend. Believe it or not, those are very hard things to teach to someone, even for us human-people!

Heh. Yeah. I guess you can say I'm pretty good at what I do . . . even for just a *regular old naked cat-thing*. Wait, that explains the two dots then.

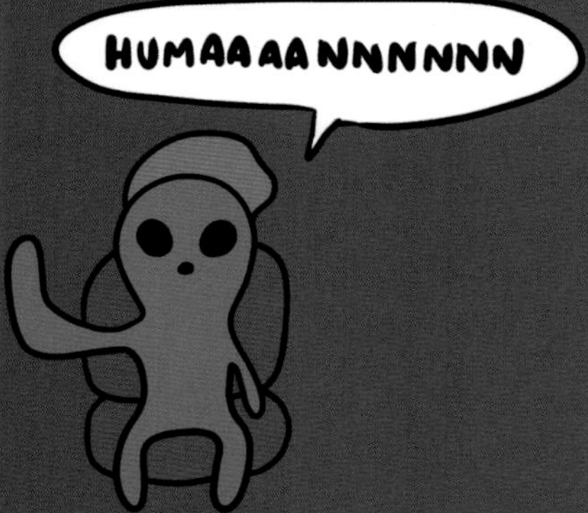
HUMAAAAANNNNNN

But I wanted to end this book on a human note . . . to say just that! YOU ARE HUMAN!

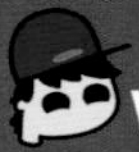

We are so lucky to be here, and I'm lucky to have had you read this book. You have been given an amazing opportunity just to exist. We shouldn't waste it by feeling down about ourselves!

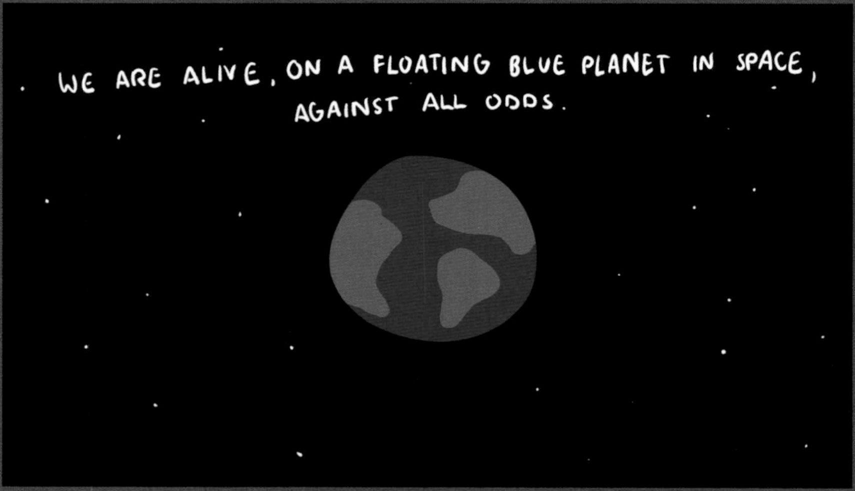
WE ARE ALIVE, ON A FLOATING BLUE PLANET IN SPACE, AGAINST ALL ODDS.

WE HAVE OPPOSABLE THUMBS, TO GRAB THINGS LIKE COFFEE AND MEATBALLS.

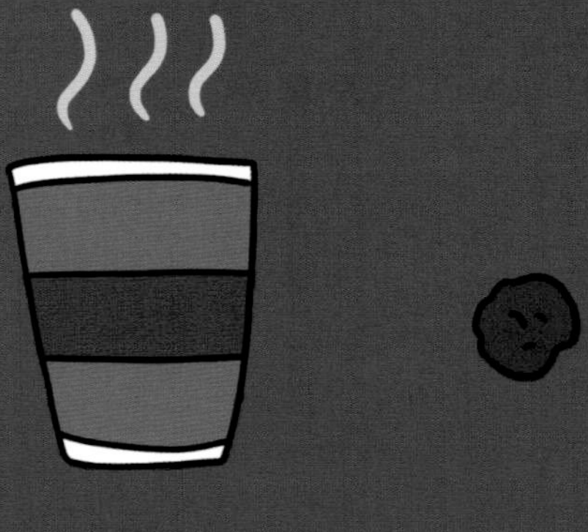

WE CAN DANCE AND SING ALL NIGHT LONG.

WE DREAM AMAZING DREAMS AND MAKE THEM BECOME REALITIES.

WE CARE AND WANT THE BEST FOR EACH OTHER, UNLIKE ANY OTHER SPECIES.

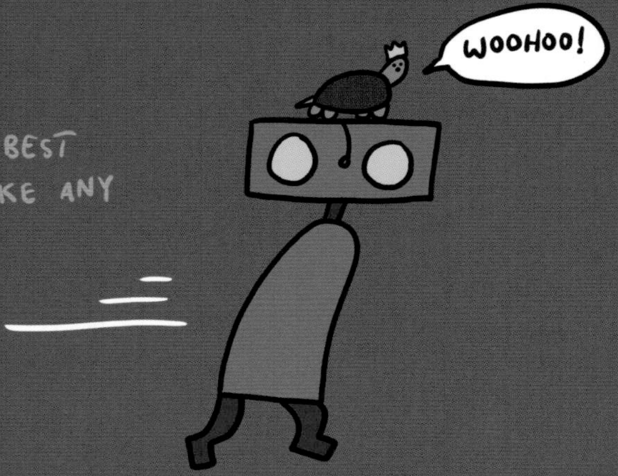
WOOHOO!

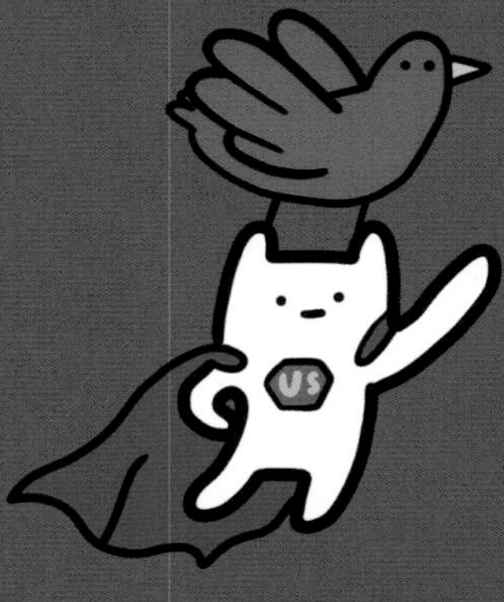
US

WE CAN DO ANYTHING WE PUT OUR MINDS TO.

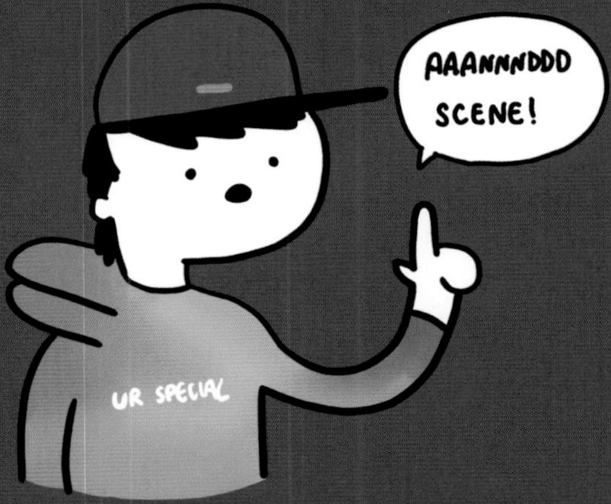
AAANNNDDD SCENE!
UR SPECIAL

We only get one chance to be here, and we might as well do it with a smile. You should love everything. You should love your friends. You should love life. And most of all, you should love yourself . . . because you are you, and you are amazing!

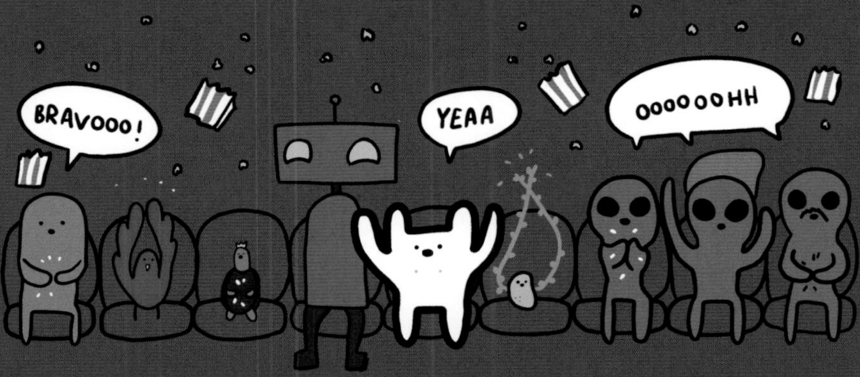
BRAVOOO!
YEAA
OOOOOOHH

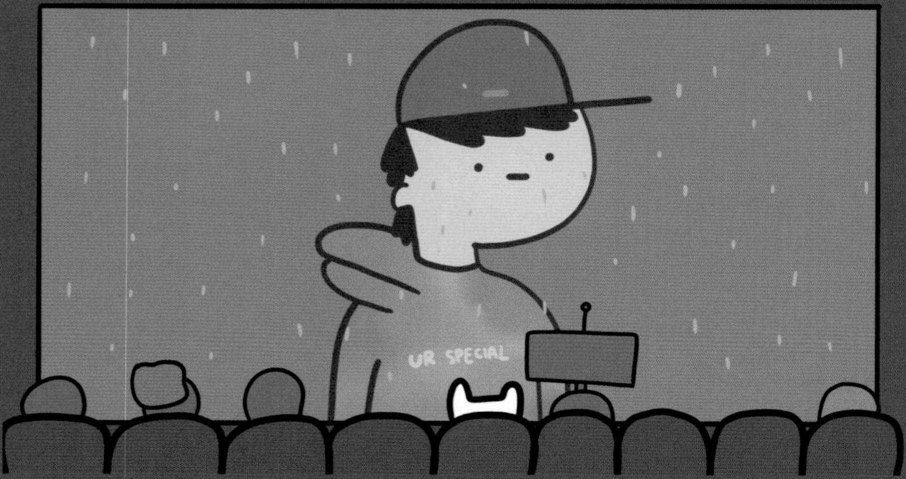
UR SPECIAL

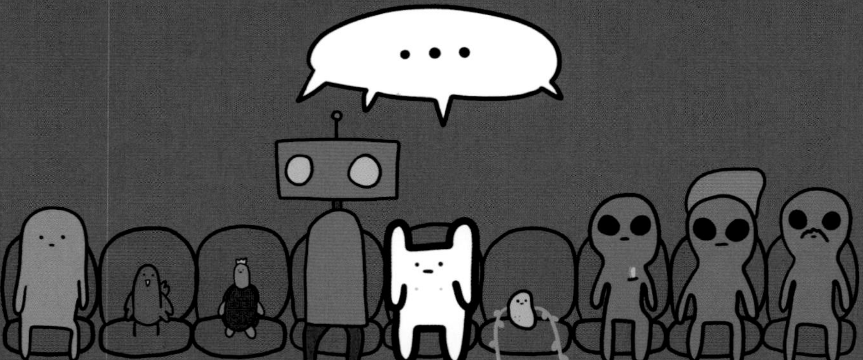
. . .

Now what?

Anybody in the mood for some ice cream?

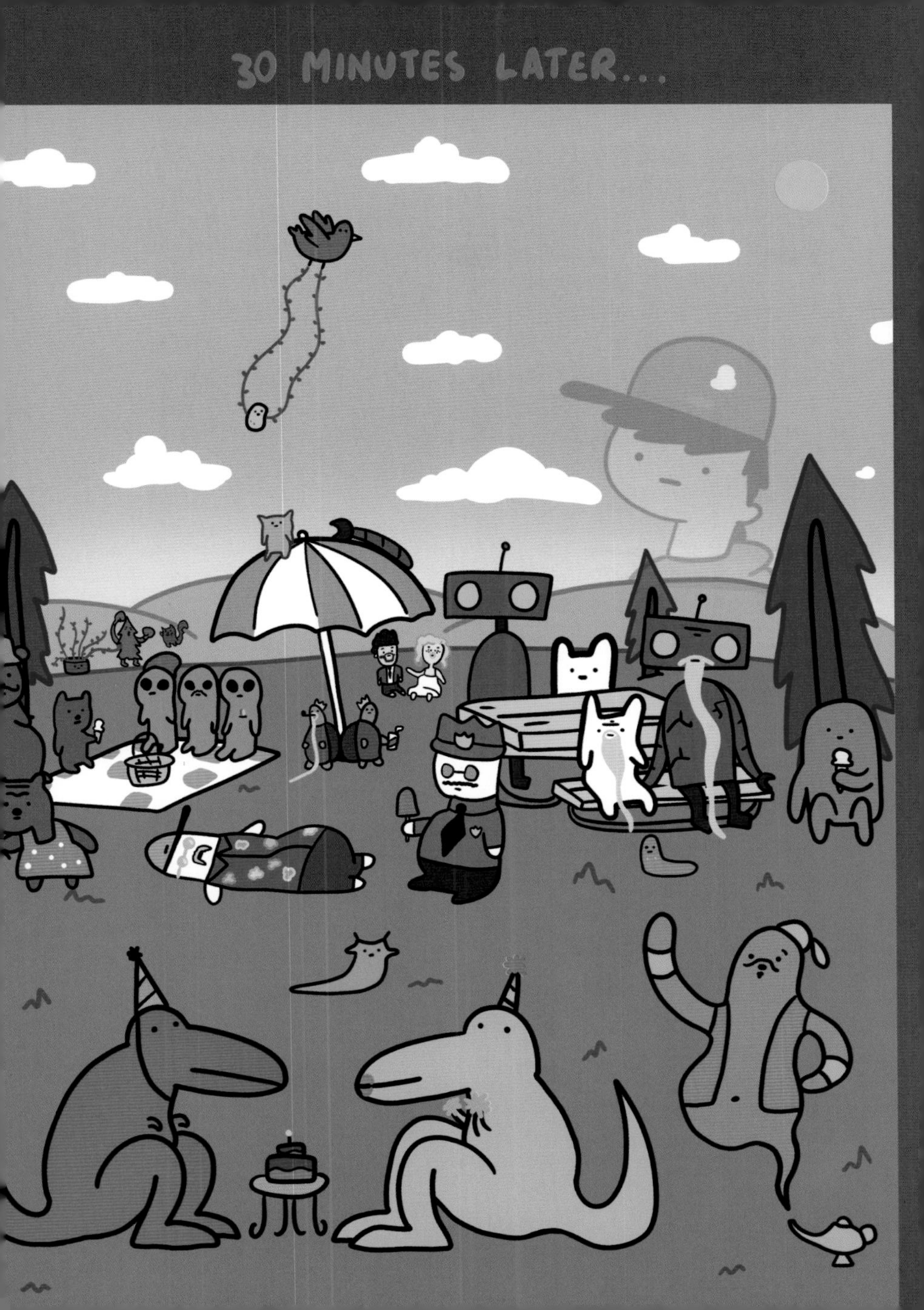

30 MINUTES LATER...

 Well, I guess we reached the end of the book. Sorry that weird human guy kind of ruined it. That's the last time I buy expensive movie tickets like that. Anyway. It was nice hanging out with you. I hope I taught you something that you can take with you after you close this book. Maybe you put this book down and pick it back up again when you feel you need it most. Or maybe you lend this book to someone you feel might benefit from its lessons and stories. Either way, take care of yourself. There's only one version of you. Even when life challenges you, and you reach some low points, it's important to remember that the world is mostly good and filled with amazing things for you to experience. And if nothing else, just keep the following fact in mind . . .

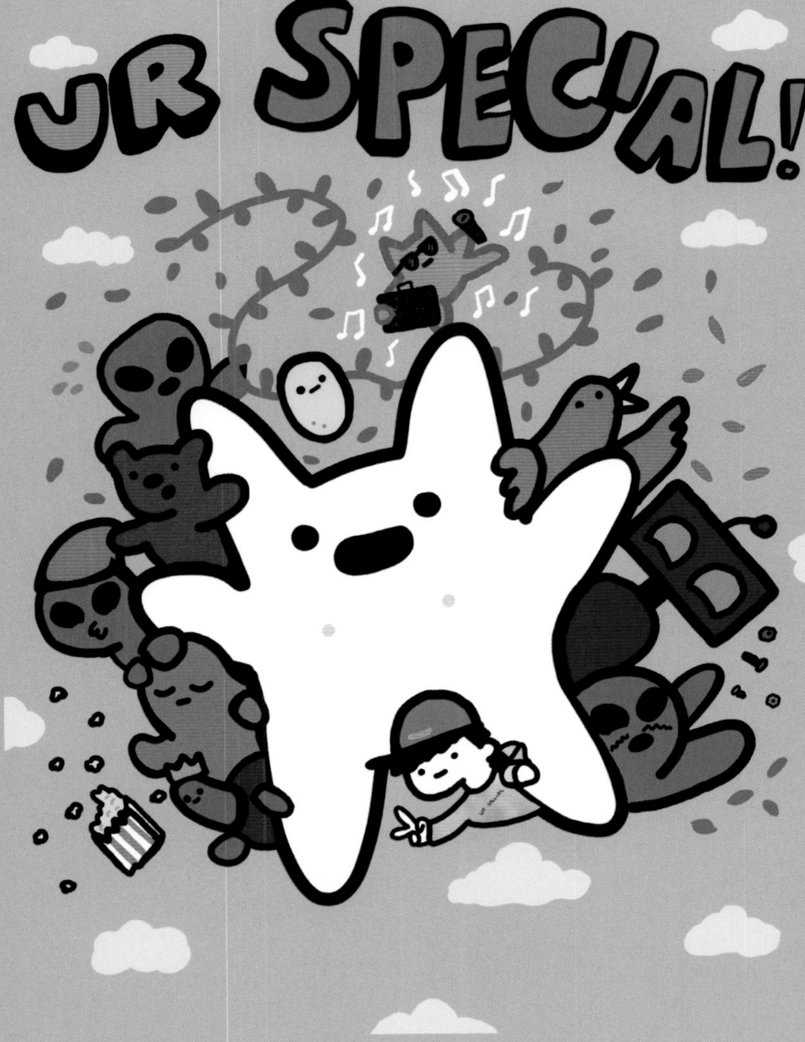
UR SPECIAL!

acknowledgments

Making this book during 2020 was an interesting adventure. With all the troubling obstacles that came with such a troubling year, this book acted as the shining star to get me through. If nothing else, art and imagination will always be there for you . . . and this book acts as a reminder of exactly that.

Thank you Mom, Dad, sister, and brothers. You always let me be myself and helped bring my ideas to life.

Thank you to my friends in New York who supported me. Life wouldn't be nearly as fun without you.

Thank you to the teachers and mentors who were always there for me. Your kindness and advice never went unnoticed or unappreciated.

Thank you to my grandma and grandpa. Proof that class, charisma, and good stories never go out of style.

Thank you to my manager, Max, and the rest of my team for seeing something in me. I'm so lucky to have such incredible representation like you.

Thank you Nigel Ng for helping design everything in this book. I mean, who wouldn't want to spend a summer coloring robots and potatoes??

Thank you Lauren Appleton and all the other amazingly talented people at Penguin Random House for making this book what it is. You allowed a weirdo like me to make a book! That's hilarious!

And last (but certainly not least) thank you to all my fans. One day in eighth-grade Spanish class, I was daydreaming how to turn my casual pastime of doodling into a full-time career. I never imagined it would happen the way it did. I'm so glad I'm able to entertain people through my dumb, simple art. It's such a dream come true, and it's all thanks to you.

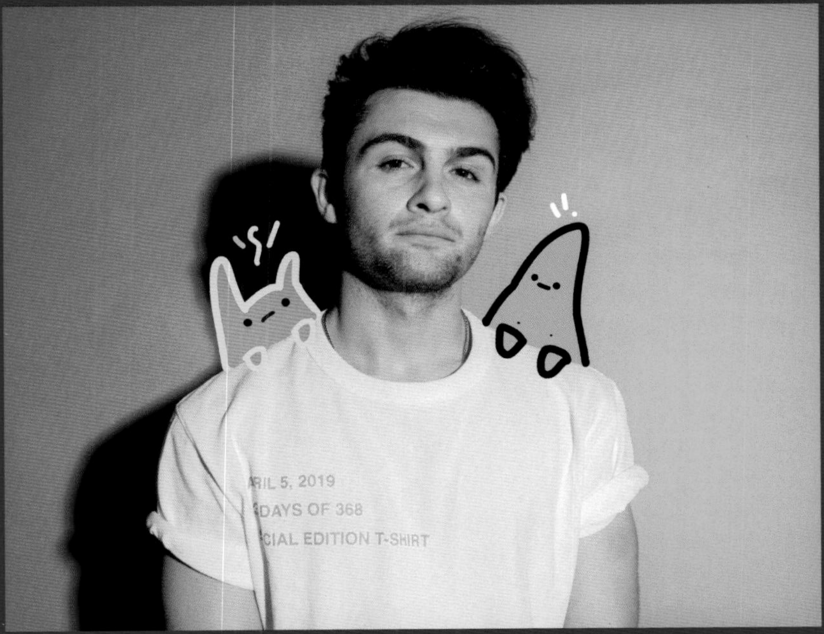
5, 2019
DAYS OF 368
EDITION T-SHIRT

about the author

Danny Casale (aka @coolman_coffeedan) is an artist in New York City who has gained popularity through his surreal, humorous, and crudely drawn animations. The self-titled "Bad Animator" first went viral in 2017 when his cartoon titled "Snakes Have Legs" accumulated tens of millions of views. Following the massive success of this video, Danny continued creating animations in his unique style, which have gone on to reach hundreds of millions more around the world . . . making them laugh, cry, and think.

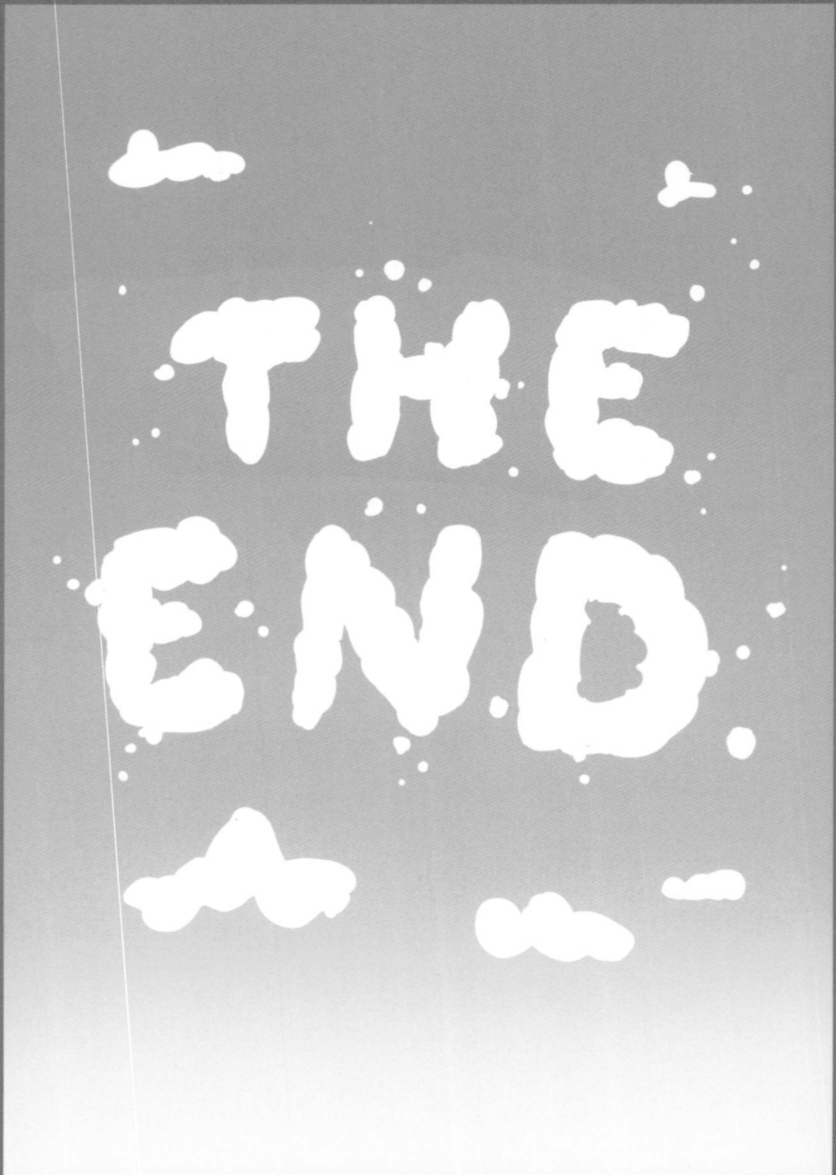
THE END